ATHERTON'S
ASHES

ATHERTON'S
ASHES

How England Won
the 2009 Ashes

Mike Atherton

SIMON &
SCHUSTER

London · New York · Sydney · Toronto

A CBS COMPANY

First published in Great Britain by Simon & Schuster UK Ltd, 2009
A CBS COMPANY

Copyright © 2009 by Mike Atherton

1 3 5 7 9 10 8 6 4 2

Simon & Schuster UK Ltd
1st Floor
222 Gray's Inn Road
London
WC1X 8HB

www.simonandschuster.co.uk

Simon & Schuster Australia
Sydney

All photos © Patrick Eagar
All statistics and scorecards by Ian Marshall

A CIP catalogue for this book is available
from the British Library.

ISBN: 978-1-84737-816-3

Typeset in Garamond by M Rules
Printed in the UK by CPI Mackays, Chatham ME5 8TD

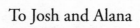

To Josh and Alana

Contents

Acknowledgements

If journalism is regarded as a low art, then sports journalism is regarded as the lowest form of a low art, and it is with this in mind that these pieces from *The Times* are, humbly, offered. It is, of course, a dangerous exercise to put one's thoughts, which are designed only for the following day and then for fish and chips, down as a permanent record. Especially, it might be said, a series such as this with its flows and contra-flows, twist and turns, plots and sub-plots.

Looking back I can see that my faith deserted me after Headingley, although in my defence I would say that I was certain before the series began that England would win. Quite how they did is still something of a mystery, Australia's batsmen scoring eight hundreds to England's two, their bowlers occupying the leading places in the wicket-takers lists. In the end, it came down to just two spells of bowling in London, one from Andrew Flintoff, one from Stuart Broad: winning the big moments are always more important than racking up decent statistics.

Sport is so emphatic in its conclusions, something that renders the opinion offered by pundits and journalists as uniquely forgettable. But if punditry is rendered quickly redundant, then there is something to be said for a record of events, of what it was like to be there, through the eyes of a disinterested observer, albeit one with his inevitable prejudices and points of view.

This, then, is a faithful record of how I felt about this series, through the daily articles written in *The Times*. Mostly, they were filed within 45 minutes of the close of play, although Friday deadlines dictated a rather more expeditious conclusion. My thanks to the outstanding subs at *The Times* who continue to save me from embarrassment, to Keith Blackmore, the Deputy Editor of *The Times*, for allowing these pieces to be reproduced, to Ian Marshall for his help in organising them into some kind of order, to Jon Holmes, whose idea this was, and to Ian Chapman at Simon and Schuster, who took the project on, bravely at a time when England and *The Times*'s correspondent were wobbling.

Writing and broadcasting almost simultaneously is immensely enjoyable, but requires a degree of understanding, so in particular I would like to thank Paul King, the Executive Producer of Sky Sports cricket coverage, for being so understanding on Fridays, when the early deadlines demand fewer commentary stints in the final session of play.

Introduction

Before the start of the Ashes series, I did a strange thing. I drove to Lord's on a non-cricket day, parked behind the museum, went in, and looked upon the Ashes for the first time. I knew what they looked like, of course (which English or Australian cricketer doesn't?), but I had never set eyes upon the urn itself, nor, really, thought too much about what it represents.

This is odd, is it not? The only day of Test cricket I went to before I became a Test cricketer myself was an Ashes match. *The* Ashes match, if you like, 'Botham's Ashes' of 1981. Actually, the day I was at Headingley was a rather dull affair, John Dyson grinding out a worthy if utterly unmemorable hundred. But, days later, I can remember standing outside a Rediffusion shop in the middle of Manchester, watching a television through a window with a crowd of people as Bob Willis completed that remarkable victory. Then, later with my family on holiday in France, I remember sitting at Le Havre, waiting for a ferry, listening on the radio as the Edgbaston match of that series reached its thrilling climax.

It was the Ashes that got me hooked, really hooked, on cricket, and I went on to play in seven Ashes series, it must be said, without any great success. Truth be told, I never thought that much about what I was playing for: the contest in itself was enough. At that time, Australia were without question the best team in the world; they had a number of undeniably great cricketers, against whom it was a privilege to play, and that was what I was playing for: to test myself and the team I represented against the best. The Ashes never really came into it – and I never got hold of them.

Standing in the Lord's museum in front of the urn, in its Perspex box with a solitary light illuminating the fading words, gave me a chance to think about all the fuss. Funny, a Perspex box was the focus of much attention at Lord's last year, too. Allen Stanford, then described as a Texan billionaire, now as an alleged fraudster, brought a Perspex box with him stuffed with dollars, 20 million's worth of them. He thought he could buy cricket. What he bought was the acquiescence of administrators with a feel for money, but not the game, and cricketers happy to play a meaningless game for a fast buck.

What he couldn't buy was meaning and context. That can only come with the passage of time. I suppose the urn, then, has two meanings: one, physical; the other, symbolic. The physical urn, so cherished by the MCC, is important only in terms of its value as an historical artefact and because of its place at the start of what has become a remarkable narrative. When Ivo Bligh accepted a small terracotta urn from his future wife at a country game just outside Melbourne, how could he have known how much agony, grief and joy it would produce?

Much more important than the physical urn, though, is the symbolic, what I referred to and thought of as the contest against the best, and what it came to mean to countless others who have played in England–Australia contests. The Ashes are as much about Australia as England, a chance for them to show that their system is stronger than ours, which results over the last 50 years would suggest it is. It also gives an opportunity for the kind of needle we all know exists between the two countries to be expressed; needle best outlined by the Australian philosopher David Stove 30 years ago. 'The margin of superiority is slight,' he wrote, 'but it is consistent and therefore calls for an explanation . . . My own belief is that it is due to a difference in attitude towards the opponent: that whereas the Australians hate the Poms, the Poms only despise the Australians.'

In recent times, partly due to Steve Waugh's keen sense of history, Australia have always been better at calling upon historical antecedents as a way of inspiring and motivating. So it was that before the 2009 Ashes, every touring Australian was asked to speak to the group about what the Ashes meant to him. Michael Clarke, ever the modern player, gave a power-point presentation, replete with images of past Australian glories; Ricky Ponting spoke straightforwardly about the day his uncle Greg Campbell got called up to the Australian team for the 1989 Ashes tour, and Ponting got to see and feel the Australian cap and all the rest of the clobber for the first time. Simon Katich recalled the days of his youth watching Terry Alderman dismantle Graham Gooch in 1989, and so on. This was a team attempting to understand what I was trying to understand when I went to Lord's to see the Ashes.

For 16 years, between 1989 and 2005, the Ashes had lost its significance as an arbiter of where the balance of power lay in the cricketing world. Not that, with the rise of India, the 2005 series necessarily solved that question, but with the Ashes now a contest rather than a procession, interest began to register again. Never mind that the never-to-be-mentioned 2006–07 series suggested a return to one-sided ways, but the twists and turns of the 'greatest series ever played', as the 2005 series soon became known, whetted the appetite once more.

And there was enough evidence to suggest that the 2009 version would be another close-run thing. The biggest factor in this supposition was not England's improvement following the whitewash of 2006–07, but the inevitable break-up of one of the greatest winning machines that cricket has known. It was always going to be Ricky Ponting's lot to be in charge when that happened, and a look around his squad on the eve of departure would have confirmed to him what Andrew Strauss would eventually refer to as a 'loss of aura'.

Gone were Matthew Hayden, Justin Langer, Adam Gilchrist, Damien Martyn, Jason Gillespie and, most tellingly of all, Shane Warne and Glenn McGrath. Nobody had done more than the last two named to ensure Australian dominance of the previous 15 years, but the only cricket both were playing now was in the lucrative Indian Premier League, although McGrath couldn't even get a gig for his team in that. The IPL had also hoovered up Hayden and Gilchrist, too, while Langer continued to ply his trade in the LV County Championship for Somerset.

Langer was Australia's spy in the camp. Before the series, Tim Nielsen, Australia's coach, asked Langer for a dossier on England's players and English cricket in general and he supplied what came to be an explosive document when it was released during the Headingley Test. In it he suggested that England are great front runners, but that they quickly go 'flat and lazy' when things get tough. 'English players rarely believe in themselves,' he wrote. 'Many of them stare a lot and chat a lot but this is very shallow . . . they will retreat very quickly. Aggressive batting, running and body language will soon have them staring at their bootlaces rather than in the eyes of their opponents.' All good stuff – not that these contests need any outside influences to stir the blood.

Langer's focus was on England, but Ponting's would have been on his own team. Whereas the 2005 Australia team contained eight cricketers on their third tour of England, the 2009 squad had just Ponting himself, Brett Lee, Simon Katich and Michael Clarke with Ashes experience in England. There were new faces everywhere he looked: Mitchell Johnson, Peter Siddle, Ben Hilfenhaus represented a green-as-grass attack, while Phillip Hughes, the young opener from banana country, was touted as a genius but had played only a handful of Test matches. The Australian selectors clearly had a remarkable degree of faith in him, because they chose not to select a reserve opener.

For the first time in many years, it was possible to argue that England had more world-class players (Andrew Flintoff and Kevin Pietersen over Ricky Ponting), more talent generally and fewer weaknesses. The yawning gap in Australia's squad was its startling lack of spin options. Shane Warne's dominance during the 1990s and 2000s was supposed to have encouraged a whole new generation to take up spin, but within two years of Warne's retirement, there was room for only one spinner in the squad, and that a finger-spinner, too, by the name of Nathan Hauritz, who was taking his wickets at the unhealthy average of 48 in state cricket. England, having chosen Cardiff as the venue for the first Test, anticipated a fruitful summer if the weather stayed dry and the pitches turned.

Most of the pre-tour attention focused on Hughes and Johnson. Hughes had been given an opportunity by Middlesex to experience English conditions, a decision seen as treacherous in some quarters. The way he flayed second division bowlers around suggested we were witnessing another genius from the outback, but it also gave Andrew Strauss an opportunity to look at Hughes's eccentric technique from close quarters. Johnson, meanwhile, was expected the lead the attack with the kind of menace and hostility he had displayed in South Africa. If Australia were to prosper, it was vital that players such as these, whose promise outweighed achievement, settled quickly.

There were some collateral form lines to be considered, all of which involved South Africa. England had been beaten the previous summer by Graeme Smith's team, although the final result failed to reflect the closeness of the contest. Australia, meanwhile, had been beaten at home by South Africa but then triumphed away. In the first of those series, Duncan Fletcher, the former England coach who was now 'consulting' with South Africa, reckoned Australian cricket to be on its knees, at its lowest ebb since the mid-1980s.

But Australian cricket has a remarkable ability to regenerate quickly, and the way Ponting's team turned the tables in South Africa suggested that England would have to play very well to win. The secret of Australia's turnaround? It was almost as if they had rediscovered their soul: backing some young, unproven players who, said Ponting, had given the team renewed energy and vibrancy. Where an Englishman sees inexperience, Australians see promise.

Since 2006–07, England had gone through a period of turbulence. Duncan Fletcher's outstanding tenure came to a bitter and acrimonious end during the World Cup in the Caribbean, and those charged with running the English game slipped the unproven, inexperienced Peter Moores into the job without opening it up to outside candidates. Moores had long been identified as Fletcher's successor, based on his achievements with Sussex, but he had precious little knowledge or understanding of international cricket.

Moores's tenure was an unsuccessful one. Crucially, he failed to establish good relationships with his senior players, so that, during the South Africa series in 2008, he lost not one but two captains, Michael Vaughan relinquishing the Test captaincy, and Paul Collingwood the one-day job. Kevin Pietersen, who had severe doubts about Moores's ability to do the job, was offered both roles, which, after a lengthy discussion with the coach, he accepted.

Pietersen's doubts, though, could not be shaken off and after a disappointing tour of India, which saw England beaten in the Test and one-day series, Pietersen sent a confidential memo to the England and Wales Cricket Board, outlining his concerns. Once his thoughts were leaked to a national newspaper, the story ran out of control and within weeks of the beginning of 2009,

England had a new captain, Andrew Strauss, and a new coach, Andy Flower. This was far from ideal preparation, just six months before the Ashes were due to get underway.

Strauss and Flower, though, were cut from very different cloth to Moores and Pietersen. Strauss was calmer, less prone to mood swings, if lacking some of Pietersen's intuitiveness. Flower, who had kept a low profile as assistant coach to Moores, suddenly came into his own, speaking openly, honestly and directly about England's problems and quickly gaining the respect of the players and close observers alike.

Not that success came easily, or at all, in the Caribbean. A disastrous second-innings performance in Jamaica, which saw England shot out for 51, was enough to seal a series defeat. But, in the games that followed, it was clear that the team was enjoying the new-found stability at the helm. Strauss himself clearly enjoyed the extra responsibility, batting better than at any other time in his career.

What England badly needed before the Ashes was the experience of winning again, and a gilt-edged opportunity presented itself with the arrival of the West Indies for two early-season Tests at Lord's and the Riverside, Chester-le-Street. The West Indies were duly brushed aside by ten wickets and an innings and 83 runs, with hundreds for Ravi Bopara, who had now scored three consecutive centuries in Tests, and five-wicket hauls for Graham Onions, the wiry Durham bowler who debuted at Lord's, and James Anderson.

England, then, approached the Ashes series with a degree of confidence, although, like Australia, it was a very different team from the one that had won so thrillingly four years before. Only

Andrew Flintoff remained of the 'fab four' bowling attack, with Stephen Harmison out of favour, Matthew Hoggard past his best and Simon Jones, cruelly, still injured. The biggest echo of 2005, though, came just before the series began when the architect of England's triumph, Michael Vaughan, decided to cut short his attempts to regain his place. His retirement was touted as an exercise in selflessness, but in reality it reflected little more than the passage of time. Vaughan had been an outstanding captain and batsman, but would watch this Ashes series from the comfort of the hospitality boxes.

The World Twenty20, which preceded the Ashes, was a triumph for the ECB, but it told us little about which direction the Ashes winds would blow. England were predictably poor, losing an astonishing match to the Netherlands in the opening fixture of the tournament. Australia looked equally rusty and failed to make it past the opening exchanges and were forced to spend more time than they might have liked in Leicestershire while the knockout stages were completed. Predictably, Australia saw an advantage in their early elimination in that it gave them a chance to spend quality time practising their long-game skills.

The Twenty20 revolution provided both an interesting and disturbing backdrop to the Ashes, another reason why a re-run of something similar to 2005 would have been appreciated by those with an interest in preserving the game's status quo. Chris Gayle, the West Indies captain, had missed his team's opening fixtures of their tour so that he could complete his IPL commitments –

as had Daniel Vettori the year before – and given himself minimal preparation time before the first Test at Lord's. In an interview before the second Test, he became the first international captain to say openly what many players were privately thinking: that a fast buck made in three hours was preferable to a lesser pay cheque made over five days of hard grind.

For England, the IPL had other serious implications, particularly concerning their alpha male players, Kevin Pietersen and Andrew Flintoff. Much against what was popularly considered to be the ECB's better judgement, England had allowed their players a three-week window to play in India, insisting that they return home in good time for the start of the West Indies series. It seemed at the time a particularly poor piece of planning, especially as the players were being paid handsomely through their central contracts, and given Flintoff's particularly poor injury record. Australia's players had, by and large, taken a collective decision to turn down the IPL loot, so that they would be at their freshest, physically and mentally, for the Ashes. They had their priorities right.

Sure enough, Flintoff returned from the IPL with a torn cartilage and missed both the West Indies Test matches and the World Twenty20, although his fitness for the start of the Ashes was never in doubt. Flintoff's knee would prove to be a running story throughout the series. Not just his knee, either. When Flintoff did return to the England team, his first assignment was to visit the war graves of the fallen in France, as part of a team-building exercise. Flintoff had a late night before the trip to the war graves and duly missed the team bus. Controversy would be never far away.

Pietersen, too, returned from the IPL under an injury cloud. Excessive road-running in the Caribbean had put undue strain on his Achilles' tendon, and, ridiculously, he was allowed to go and play in the IPL when rest and recuperation would surely have been the more sensible option. The Chennai Super Kings rupee was a bigger attraction for Pietersen than taking a break, although whether he gained in the long term, given what happened during the series, is a moot point.

The game as a whole, then, needed a compelling Ashes series in order for it to realign its priorities. England's administrators, too, were praying for a rousing Ashes: they had suffered a bruising 2008, what with the Allen Stanford fiasco and the disorderly procession of England captains and coaches coming and going.

Australia warmed up for the first Test at Hove and Worcester, where the limitations of their bowling attack were highlighted. Brett Lee looked the likeliest match-winner at Worcester, where the Australians played against the England Lions, but it transpired that during the course of that game he had pulled an intercostal muscle and would miss the opening Test. England, meanwhile, had taken themselves off to Edgbaston, where Warwickshire provided suitably flimsy opposition. All roads led to Cardiff in the second week of July.

1

The Build-up to the Ashes

With an Ashes summer looming, cricket will be at the centre of the nation's sporting consciousness, which is perhaps why there has been so much introspection about how it is being run. Of all sports, cricket is prone to the greatest bouts of nostalgia. Somehow, heroes were more heroic in black and white, at the same time as the grass grew greener. The modern game, meanwhile, lurches seemingly from crisis to crisis, venal administrators and mercenary players, flitting from team to team, complicit in changing utterly the character of the game.

It is all nonsense, of course. Cricket has always confronted crisis – matchfixing pre-dated Hansie Cronje by a century and a half – and adapted to meet the demands of the age, and players have always had an eye on the bottom line. When an audacious Lancashire League club tried to capture the services of Don Bradman in 1931, its secretary was moved to complain that 'the voice at the Sydney end of the line was that of a cool, calculating young man who is out to hit iron while it is hot.'

It is a resilient game, as the editor of *Wisden* noted this year in the Almanack: in spite of everything, he wrote, 'the fundamental fun of bat and ball remains unchanged . . . the play as absorbing, the teas as delicious, the banter as witty, the drinks as refreshing.' It is, he added: 'An astonishing, unique game in all its forms' and one that has 'regenerated and grown over the centuries as no other sport has done'. Little argument there.

Nevertheless, it would be hard to imagine a more difficult year than the one administrators of the game have just shambled their way through. Certainly, John Woodcock, the longest-serving cricket correspondent of *The Times*, could think of no other year that presented such serious challenges: the Twenty20 revolution and the stampede to profit from it without any clear plan how to do so; the Stanford fiasco; the problem of the Indian Cricket League; the Mumbai terror attacks; the atrocity in Lahore involving the Sri Lanka team; an abandoned Test match in the Caribbean; and, for England, the loss of three captains and a head coach and paltry returns on the field.

We are always on hand to criticise, but seldom acknowledge the difficulties. At board level, the feeling persists, apparently, that the numerous detractors of the England and Wales Cricket Board (ECB) are too swift to pounce on errors and insufficiently understanding of the problems. Hence the recent debate as to whether more professional PR help should be utilised (Max Clifford was mentioned in dispatches).

There was the odd administrative triumph last year, such as the cute manoeuvring after the bombings in Mumbai and the subsequent return to India, which has put Indian cricket in the ECB's debt, and Giles Clarke's Lalit Modi-like refusal to accept defeat once the second Test against West Indies had been abandoned in Antigua. But Stanford remains the most spectacular misjudging of the public mood that I can remember and, because the England team represent you and me and several million others, it is a mood that should be noted and acted upon. No amount of professional PR could salvage that.

For that reason, above all others, the feeling grew last year that the game was being driven not by a safe pair of hands, but by a teenage joyrider under the influence of a wild cocktail of drugs. Not many would be given a second opportunity to repair such damage, but the 2009 season represents a golden one for Clarke, the ECB chairman, and his organisation. With the Ashes and the World Twenty20, the best of old and new, the ECB has the chance to showcase English cricket at a time when there are no other significant sporting distractions. No football World Cup, Olympics or Commonwealth Games – truly a summer of cricket.

With reward comes risk, though. With all eyes on English cricket, it cannot afford to waste such an opportunity. The past two major competitions that English cricket organised – the World Cup in 1999 and the Champions Trophy five years later – were efficient but unspectacular. The end-of-season weather and uncompetitive teams like the United States hampered the Champions Trophy, while the World Cup never quite recovered from the embarrassment of the opening ceremony, a few lacklustre fireworks covering Lord's with acrid smoke, nor was it helped by a typically inept performance by the hosts. Given all that, it would be preferable if the first Ashes Test was not scheduled to be hosted by a virgin international ground.

The ECB has done its best, though, to present the opportunities on offer with a whizzy marketing campaign, entitled the

Great Exhibition. The colourful logo, based on the wagon wheel of Kevin Pietersen's 158 at The Oval (did he really hit that many on the off side?), is designed to recreate the heady euphoria of 2005 and is based on a synergy (I think that's the correct marketing term) of all formats of the game, players of all abilities and spectators of all persuasions.

There will be giant screens in Southampton, Liverpool, Cambridge, Derby and London during the Ashes series, cut-price tickets throughout the summer – and with unemployment passing the two million mark yesterday, there is a ready-made LV County Championship audience – and free coaching clinics. With the emphasis on inclusiveness and a broad appeal, the ECB's early summer campaign – along with statistics released yesterday that boasted participation in the game has increased year on year by 24 per cent overall and 33 per cent among five- to 16-year-olds – is doing its best to put the embarrassment of 2008 behind it. A return to values based on enjoyment and participation, rather than naked exploitation, is welcome.

As ever, though, success or otherwise of the season will be determined by what happens on the field. Almost as if in tune with the ECB's more sensitive, sober approach, England have found themselves, by accident rather than design, with a captain and team director who could not be more distant from the abiding image of 2008, that of Stanford's helicopter landing at Lord's.

Honesty, decency and modesty were qualities notable by their absence that day, but they are qualities that spring to mind when you think of the two Andrews, Strauss and Flower. In this important year for English cricket, when it could either produce a Great Exhibition or make an exhibition of itself, they feel like men in whom to have faith.

Those dangers to the balance and structure of the game, with such an overcrowded calendar, became clear even before the season had got fully under way, with the Indian Premier League (IPL) having an unexpected impact on England's Ashes hopes. Andrew Flintoff's humbling IPL experience got a whole lot worse in late April when he flew home for keyhole surgery on his right knee. Scans revealed a 'slight medial meniscus tear' and the prognosis, given successful surgery, is a three- to five-week lay-off. He will miss the opening two npower Test matches of the summer against West Indies.

Already cast in an unfavourable light after a series of expensive bowling displays, Flintoff – jointly with Kevin Pietersen the IPL's highest-paid player with an auction fee of $1.55 million (about £1.05 million) – felt a niggle in his right knee at a practice session with the Chennai Super Kings, but felt fit enough to play against the Delhi Daredevils the next day. It turned out to be a bad day for his pride and his body: the most expensive bowling analysis in IPL history on the pitch, nought for 50 in four overs, was inflamed by further knee trouble off it, resulting in scans analysed by Nick Pierce, the ECB's chief medical officer, who recommended surgery. So, having played three of the six games to which he was contracted, his IPL adventure is over, although it is understood he will keep his full £450,000 fee.

Flintoff's principal employer, the England and Wales Cricket

Board, was quick to go on damage-limitation mode, no doubt expecting the flak that inevitably will come its way, given the widespread feeling that England's best players – like those of Australia – should be resting, or preparing for an Ashes summer with first-class cricket in England rather than Twenty20 in India. Pierce emphasised that such a degenerative injury could have happened 'any time, anywhere' (for that read, he could still have been injured playing for Lancashire).

Hugh Morris, the managing director of England cricket, found a way to put some positive spin on the situation by implying the timing of the injury was almost fortuitous, given that Flintoff will now be available for the Ashes and the World Twenty20. By doing so, Morris not only highlighted England's disregard for West Indies again, but also attempted to divert attention from his controversial decision to allow England's players to compete in the IPL, which has been widely criticised.

Pierce may well be correct to imply that Flintoff could have been injured just as easily playing for Lancashire, but would he have been tearing around the outfield at Hove, sliding on his injured right knee to save a boundary, as he was in Durban? In any case, getting injured playing for the Chennai Super Kings, instead of Lancashire or England, somehow makes things worse.

Given the player's appalling injury record and contractual situation, the ECB had every reason and right to prevent him from playing, but by cravenly capitulating to the demands of the players and the Professional Cricketers' Association, it immediately rendered worthless the central contracts – the point of which is to prevent exactly this type of thing happening. The ECB and Morris deserve all the criticism that will be thrown at them.

They will argue that they were powerless to prevent an exodus in the face of the growing influence and monetary might of the IPL. But the players are under contract to England for a reason, and are well remunerated for a reason. The ECB ought to have asked a simple question of those who wanted to go and play in the IPL: do you want to be an England centrally contracted player or a free agent? You cannot have it both ways.

Despite Morris's assurances, there is no guarantee that Flintoff will be fit for the start of the World Twenty20 in the first week of June. Surgery can go wrong and, being the type of bowler he is, Flintoff is always more prone to other injuries after a long layoff. Last summer, after recovering from an ankle injury, he immediately tore an intercostal muscle because his body had become soft from lack of bowling.

There is usually a high degree of sympathy when a player gets injured, particularly one as amiable and important as Flintoff, but in this instance any sympathy is tempered by the context. Flintoff is an extremely wealthy man and if, as he constantly assures us, England are his first priority, he did not need to take the rupee. As for Morris and the ECB, they will discover a whole raft of people – correspondents, columnists, pundits and punters – who would be well within their rights to scream: 'We told you so.'

However, it is not simply a question of the demands that the IPL places on players that is having an impact. It is also, perhaps inevitably, a question of money, for this is where the IPL has truly changed the parameters for the players. In the era I played, the extent of 'negotiations' for a new deal with Lancashire would have been a contract arriving by first-class post at the end of the season, returned, dutifully signed and unread, the next day. An agent, previously an appendage to a chosen few, is now an accepted part of the negotiating process for most first-class crick-eters, even if the suspicion remains that for many they are regarded, like a sponsored car, as little more than an indicator that a player has somehow 'arrived'.

For the most part, agents have been good news for players, and not just financially. The role played by Neil Fairbrother and Andrew 'Chubby' Chandler in helping Andrew Flintoff to get through his early demons in international cricket, by giving him some home truths and a detailed path to follow, was a triumph for the kind of holistic approach the profession has not always been noted for.

But it needs to be remembered, always, that an agent has his client's best interests at heart and that, often, those interests run counter to the best interests of the game and the people who support it. Through comments in a Sunday newspaper, Chandler recently outlined his vision for the future of England's top cricketers. He prophesied that central contracts would become a hindrance to maximising a player's earning potential and that the day would soon be upon us when a player turned down a central contract to become a free agent. Then he could play, as a priority, five or six Twenty20 tournaments a year, with England commitments fitting around them.

Chandler is not the first to work out that the natural endgame of the Indian Premier League (IPL) is the weakening of national loyalties. But nobody, I suspect, would have any problem if Flintoff or Kevin Pietersen turned down a central contract in September, allowing them freedom at the expense of guaranteed pay when injured and all the other fringe benefits – car, pension, time away from county cricket – that come with being an England player. Which dotted line a player puts his moniker on is entirely his prerogative.

What people would object to strenuously is the thought that cricketers will be able to pick and choose their destinations according to the quality of beaches or the excellence of the wine list, and that the cricket calendar will be made up of a whole host of slightly irrelevant Twenty20 tournaments in the United States or wherever, with players becoming highly paid wanderers with no ties to any club, country or community.

If international cricket is to remain the dominant form of the game, administrators have to be much stronger than they have been in the two years since the launch of the IPL. When Duncan Fletcher, the former England head coach, suggested that an abolition of central contracts would be a cop-out from an organisation without the balls to stand up to player power, he was reflecting upon the capitulation in the winter that allowed players the kind of unprecedented freedom that will mean England having to do without Flintoff in the first Test against West Indies at Lord's, and which means that Paul Collingwood is playing a Test without any match practice for a month.

You cannot force players to sign a contract against their wishes. There is, though, a simple alternative. The ECB should allow players to become free agents if they so wish, but it needs to make it clear that if any player – Pietersen, Flintoff, whoever –

chooses to represent any other team while England are playing, they will never be selected for the national team again.

What the ECB has failed to realise is that, while international cricket remains the dominant form of the game, a player's value is generated by his performances for his country. It is why, for example, Graham Napier was paid a fraction of what it cost the Royal Challengers Bangalore to sign Pietersen, who, arguably, is an inferior Twenty20 player. Pietersen's value in the IPL is based on his Test and one-day performances for England.

As soon as the ECB makes it clear that picking and choosing is not an option, that playing for England remains an honour and a commitment rather than a negotiation, the number of players wanting to turn down a central contract would diminish. Only those at the end of their careers, reputations made but unwilling any longer to put up with the grind of touring and happy to see out their careers playing festival cricket without any real meaning, would choose such an option. And because fresh blood is an essential part of the cycle of sport, those players would not be missed at all.

Commitment to the cause takes many forms, and the way in which a player looks after his body has never been considered more important than it is now. 'We don't request a player be fit, we demand it,' Geoff Miller, the national selector, said, after announcing that Samit Patel had missed out again on being selected for the England squad because of his failure to hit acceptable fitness standards.

The only dissenting voice I heard was from a former England player with whom I happened to be dining on the evening of Patel's fall from grace. As he tucked into hanger steak, fried scallions, French fries and an assortment of mustards, this former player – who was no porker in his day, but who now carries an extra pound or two – thought Patel's non-selection a disgrace. It doesn't matter how unfit he is, was the argument, you can see in his eyes that he is a competitor and that out in the middle where it counts – not in the gym where it doesn't – he is worth his place.

It is the same argument used by those who railed against David Gower's non-selection to India in 1992–93. Then, the argument was not really about Gower – great player that he was – it was about the future direction of English cricket. Graham Gooch and Gower represented polar opposites and it was the Gower camp whose voices, if not its power to change anything, held sway.

This week, by contrast, there was an utter lack of sympathy for Patel and the silence that followed his non-selection showed how far English cricket has travelled in the last two decades. We might not be any good now, but at least we are professional.

I am an alcoholic. At least I had to sign a form saying I was. Twice, actually. The first time was when England toured Pakistan during the 1996 World Cup, the second when we went to the same country five years later. To get a drink in the bar at the Pearl Continental in Peshawar (tragically obliterated in June by a bomb), I had to sign a form admitting to alcoholism. So did everyone else who wanted a drink. A team full of alcoholics! No wonder we were no good.

Am I alone in thinking that there is something deeply ambivalent about cricket's – sport's – attitude to alcohol? It is almost impossible to be part of the game, either as player or spectator, and not realise how central booze is to the whole thing. Even if you don't drink you can't escape it: you're either sitting in the stands fearful that some piss-artist is about to drop a stack of beer on your head, or you're in the dressing room feeling like a bit like a virgin in a brothel.

Actually, in Andrew Symonds's case, it is the other way round. He's the hooker in a team full of virgins; the drinker in a team full of people who don't drink. In the end, it proved to be an impossible situation for him and his team. Eager to watch his favourite rugby league team, he broke the terms of his personal contract with Cricket Australia (CA) and was seen drinking in public – not drunk, just drinking in public – and was summarily dismissed. It will prove to be the last in a long list of misdemeanours as an Australian cricketer because Symonds's international career is now all but over.

There was a poignant photo of Symonds in *The Times* after he had been dismissed, baggy-eyed and empty glass in hand, watching rugby back home in Queensland. It wasn't a pretty picture and the puffiness around the eyes might have suggested he was on another bender; more likely it reflected a man coming to terms with the fact that his life as an international sportsman is over, brought to a shuddering halt by a number of drinking-related indiscretions over the years, the latest of which would have been the mildest of all.

Reflecting on his client's demise, Symonds's manager said: 'He did tell me that he needs to surround himself with people he can relate to.' Drinkers, in other words. Jimmy Maher, a team-mate from Queensland, put the matter another way: 'It's no surprise he did well in the Indian Premier League under the stewardship of Darren Lehmann and Adam Gilchrist. These are guys who work on the adage that you train hard and play hard and enjoy yourself. Now, when he mentions having a beer, some of the new generation look at him like he's from another planet.'

It is true that Symonds has, for some time, been on the kind of slippery slope that Paul McGrath (and countless others, like Tony Adams) described in his memoir of his time as a professional footballer, when booze became not just an enabler of good times but an emasculator of everything else. At Manchester United during Ron Atkinson's time as manager in the 1980s, beer was as much a part of life as pasta is now. 'Drink offered escapism,' wrote McGrath, 'and in no time I became an expert at escaping everything around me.'

Cricket Australia will argue, then, that sending Symonds home is in his best long-term interests, and it is good to know that they will continue to help him through his troubles. Certainly it can be argued, despite their missing Symonds so badly on the field during the World Twenty20, that it was in the long-term interests of the team. But wouldn't Symonds be right to be just a little confused at this moral outrage from an organisation that shows such an enthusiasm for alcohol in its commercial arrangements, and a sport that cannot rid itself of its addiction? Symonds is out of step with his team, but not the game.

In the days following his shaming there were reminders everywhere that cricket and booze are inseparable. Ricky Ponting, who raised his finger so promptly and dismissed Symonds from his presence, is a reformed drinker. A decade ago he was photographed with a shiner after a one-day international in Sydney and a night on the tiles in a 24-hour boozer called the Bourbon and Beefsteak. It wasn't his first lapse and to his great credit he admitted to an alcohol problem and hasn't let himself down in public since. Like the born-again Christian, Ponting is now a touch evangelical for Symonds's tastes.

A few days after Symonds was sent home, David Boon – looking ever more like a 'keg on legs' – waddled out at Trent Bridge to do the ceremonials before the opening delivery of the India–Bangladesh game. Boon was a fine cricketer, but is probably remembered just as fondly for his staggering feat of altitude drinking prior to competing in the 1989 Ashes – a feat that he has exploited amply in his retirement. Boon went through 52 cans of lager on the flight over, beating the 44-can record set by Rodney Marsh, who in turn had breezed past the 42-can record set by Doug Walters. Who said modern sportsmen aren't better than their predecessors?

Next time you happen to be in an international ground, watch out for the Marston's Pedigree adverts. There's Hoggy, Vaughany, Belly and little Timmy Ambrose clutching their favourite tipple. They have no choice because Marston's is the official beer of the England team – as Tetley's was for many years in the 1990s – and has recently renewed its association for three more years. 'Cricket and cask beer is the perfect match,' the marketing director of Marston's said. John Perera, the ECB's commercial director, said: 'In the last three years Marston's has been a shining example of how a commercial partnership can work to exploit a sporting association.' One more contract for the road, then.

Cricket Australia is itself not immune from taking top dollar from brewers. It boasts Victoria Bitter, a classic Australian lager (fizzy, tasteless), as a commercial partner as well as Johnnie Walker, and Wolf Blass is the official wine supplier to the Australian cricket team and CA. By the way, did you notice what Ponting was wearing on his head at the press conference when Symonds was expelled? You got it – a VB cap. VB will be adorning the Australian shirts throughout the rest of the World Twenty20 (oops, nearly forgot, they are out of this one already), the Ashes and the one-day series to follow.

Cricket and booze, booze and cricket – a long-established partnership and, for the most part, an enjoyable one. From the moment a young player is introduced to cricket, it is made clear that alcohol is a part and parcel of the game. Scored a fifty for your club side on Saturday, did you? No doubt the cap was sent round for donations from the crowd. Hope you bought a 'jug' at the bar out of the proceeds.

My favourite cricketing memory is of a long night in the Worcestershire dressing room after a memorable cup semi-final victory for Lancashire. It would be fair to say that we weren't drinking lemonade. Victories celebrated, sorrows drowned in defeat. Win or lose, let's sup some booze!

Spectators drink it and cricket organisations promote it. Most players enjoy it, too, and for many this forms part of their legend when their careers are done. 'Did you see Fred? Couldn't talk at Trafalgar Square, could he? Did you see his eyes? Piss-holes in the snow. Been on it all night. Thought he was going to drop his daughter off the top of that bus, he was so smashed. Had to have a leak in the rose bushes in Tony Blair's garden! What a legend!'

Just be careful when and where you do it. 'Have you seen what Fred's done now? Got a big match coming up and he's gone and got shedded. Can you believe it? Drinking all night till four in the morning and then fell off a pedalo. Unprofessional, that's what he is. What a disgrace.' Symonds has gone, but not the hypocrisy.

Oops, he's gone and done it again. Andrew Flintoff is back and the talk, once again, is not of cricket but of discipline, time-keeping and alcohol. A trip to Flanders designed, presumably, to broaden players' minds and get a bit of good PR has blown up in England's face with the news that Flintoff has been disciplined for missing the team bus. It is a distraction that nobody needs right now, in the week before the Ashes.

Hugh Morris, managing director of England cricket, certainly didn't need it. After a fraught winter, Morris has been enjoying a stint out of the limelight as good results and a lack of off-field crises have enabled him to go to ground. So with the Ashes just around the corner, he would have preferred not to have spent much of his time during a press conference at Edgbaston fudging the question as to whether Flintoff had been drinking heavily the night before missing the bus. If it does emerge that Flintoff was drinking, Morris will be made to look both foolish and economical with the truth. Thanks, Fred.

Andrew Strauss didn't need it. Attempting to deflect criticism from his all-rounder, he was forced to concede that what Morris called an 'alarm clock issue' is not specific to Flintoff. The team, Strauss said, have a time-keeping issue generally. Ravi Bopara is known to have missed a team meeting this summer, but from what Strauss said at the press conference, it is a more widespread challenge for his team to defeat. After that, the Aussies should be a cinch.

If true, there are three problems: it suggests a lack of respect for the leaders of the group, Andy Flower and Strauss himself, and a lack of authority on their part; it suggests a lack of respect within the group generally – is there any worse feeling than being kept waiting because of someone else's rudeness or forgetfulness? – and it makes England sound not like the national team made up of heroes but a team full of adolescents who cannot manage themselves properly.

Flintoff certainly didn't need it because, let's face it, he's got plenty of previous in this regard: there was the 'Fredalo' incident in the 2007 World Cup, the drunk in charge of practice in Australia during the 2006–07 tour and questions to be answered on his whereabouts after England were bowled out for 51 against West Indies last winter. So Freddie will spend the days before the first Test at Cardiff under scrutiny, when a pleasant run-out against Warwickshire, and headlines for cricketing reasons at last, was the order of the day.

Flower didn't need it. This latest indiscretion will inevitably raise question marks as to how far the Lancastrian is prepared to buy into the team director's regime. Throughout the winter, and again at the start of this summer, slowly but surely Flower has helped Strauss repair the damage done by a period during which the previous captain and coach, Kevin Pietersen and Peter Moores, were on a collision course.

Flintoff has not been involved for much of that time because of injury. He didn't play the final three Tests of the winter and hasn't appeared this summer because of the injury sustained in the IPL. England have been doing very well without him, thank you very much, and it is impossible to ignore the implication behind the comments that the dressing room has been a very contented place. Flower, too, will be well aware that Duncan Fletcher's authority was eroded to damaging effect after his failure to discipline Flintoff during the previous Ashes tour. Flower will not want to make that mistake – and Flintoff should be careful because Flower is no soft touch.

It was, then, the faulty alarm clock that did no one any good. Does it matter at all? That all depends on results. And there is no doubt as to who is the man with the most responsibility to ensure they are as good as possible.

I tell Andy Flower my Sir Alex Ferguson story: about how I found myself in the Manchester United changing room some years ago, minutes before the start of a critical fixture against Arsenal; about how the atmosphere was unbelievably relaxed – players playing cards, watching telly, that kind of thing; and about how Ferguson was nowhere to be seen. When I asked

Ferguson about his absence afterwards, he said that the preparations had been done days before and there was no need to be there because he had absolute faith in his team.

Flower likes the story because it chimes with his coaching philosophy, about which we are speaking to promote the Sky Sports/ECB Coach Education Programme. It is a philosophy centred on empowering players to make their own choices and raising their self-awareness. 'The more trust you place in people, I believe the more they will repay you; the better you understand yourself the better your chances of success,' the England team director said.

Although he has never said it, I suspect Flower looks at his England team and sees a bunch of narrow-minded, overly cosseted cricketers. Nobody could accuse Flower of that, coming from Zimbabwe, seeing at first hand the disintegration of a country and becoming politicised inevitably because of it. He wouldn't wish that experience on anyone, but he does want to broaden the England players' minds and help them grow as human beings.

'That was the most important aim of the trip to Flanders,' he said, reflecting on England's pre-Ashes bonding journey. 'Sometimes as cricketers you get caught up in your own little world and don't enjoy a wide enough range of experiences. We wanted to reconnect with English history a little to help the players appreciate who they are and where they fit in. We've put a lot of effort into personal growth, leadership and development programmes and Flanders was part of that. It was not Ashes specific.'

Rather than bringing the team some welcome headlines,

though, the trip turned into something of a PR disaster, with the news that one player forgot the only thing he had to remember – his passport – and that Andrew Flintoff was unable to make the team bus on time. Andrew Strauss, attempting to defend the all-rounder, was sidetracked into admitting that team discipline is not what it should be, generally. How disappointed was Flower with the fall-out?

'I know what we got out of it as a group, so we are very comfortable with that. It was a very worthwhile experience and sometimes a moving experience. I know that the perception is that it has been sullied in some way, but I'm happy with what we got from it. I'm obviously disappointed with the hullabaloo that followed because we don't want that of kind of publicity.

'In any team there are time-keeping issues because people aren't perfect. I wouldn't say we are outstandingly bad compared to other teams I've worked in. There are always issues that crop up. It is important we iron it out, though, because poor time-keeping and bad discipline are common denominators of poor teams. We also have a lot of mutual respect, cohesion and fun, which are common values in good teams.'

At this point, Flintoff is inevitably the elephant in the room. The all-rounder's ill discipline was fundamental to the slow strangulation of Duncan Fletcher's impressive stint as England coach. How far does the knowledge of that put Flower in an awkward position now? 'It doesn't, because every player starts with a clean slate and I'm not judging him on anything that went before. He made a bad mistake, but I'll tell you right now that I've made more mistakes than Andrew

Flintoff. He apologised to the team and pledged his commitment to do things well for the rest of the summer. Obviously, we had to speak to him privately about it and he has been formally warned. But that is the end of the matter for us as a team. It might come up in the press again, but we can move on.'

But will he be prepared to drop a big-name player, no matter who it is, for a significant lapse of discipline during the Ashes? 'It's a sensitive issue: I won't just say "Yes, of course I would" just because that is what everyone wants to hear. What I will say is that this particular situation was not a big enough thing for me to drop Andrew Flintoff. No way was it a serious enough issue to do that, to finish someone's career. I'm very clear in my own mind about that.

'But if a difficult decision has to be made, we will make a difficult decision. But, you know, those are often not the most difficult decisions because if someone transgresses seriously enough in your judgement, it becomes a simple decision – you just do it because it is the right thing to do for the team. All the decisions we make are in the best interests of the England cricket team; there are no hidden agendas at all – it's simple.

'In the car this morning I was listening to Ronnie Irani on the radio. Now Ronnie is an old friend from Essex, but there were some things being said on that show about how Flintoff should be axed straight away and shouldn't take any part in the Ashes. It was utterly ridiculous. We're talking about the end of someone's England career and I'm not prepared to finish someone's career on that basis. It's just crazy talk.'

Flower is about embark on the most high-profile two months of his cricketing life, but nothing in his career, either as a brilliant player for Zimbabwe or during his brief time as coach can compare with an Ashes series. Is it a fair question to ask why we should have faith in him? 'It's certainly valid. In fact, you could go further and say that playing for Zimbabwe means that I know little about winning in international cricket.

'But just because you haven't experienced a specific situation doesn't mean you cannot add value. If you took that attitude, you would never blood a young player, for example. When you break it down into its simplest version, it's about one team trying to beat another. Whether you call it the Ashes or not, that doesn't change.'

He has coached formally ever since his twenties and says that he has pinched the good bits from every coach he has worked with, and remembered some of the bad, too. He admired the no-nonsense attitude of John Hampshire, the former Yorkshire and England player who coached Zimbabwe, and his emphasis on keeping things simple and doing the basics well; there was the tactical and technical knowledge of Dave Houghton and the freedom and lack of scrutiny given to him by Carl Rackemann, both of whom also coached Zimbabwe; Graham Gooch's enthusiasm, love of the game and his work ethic at Essex; and the way Peter Moores, the previous England head coach, challenged him and made every day a joyful one. He's also met twice with John Buchanan, the former Australia coach, in the last month ('I've really enjoyed talking with him, throwing different ideas around') to pick his brains about the Australians.

Faith in himself, then, with enough experience of his own and other coaches to draw on. But, to come back to the Ferguson story, how much faith does he have in his team? 'We're some way from the Ferguson ideal, if I'm honest, because we're fifth in the world. If we were close to it, then we would be closer to number one in the world. Once we are in the position where the players are making good decisions for themselves, and making good decisions under pressure, then I assure you we will be closer to where I want us to be.

'We have a good chance this summer and I believe we can win, but I'm not about to make predictions. We're not scared of favouritism but I don't think we're favourites because they are the number one ranked team in the world. We have home advantage, though, and there are vulnerabilities in this Australian outfit that were not there before.

'They have lost a wealth of experience: Warne, Gilchrist, McGrath, Gillespie, Hayden and Langer. Any side losing those sorts of people is going to be weakened. Some of those guys were once-a-generation players, great characters on the field and in the dressing room. We certainly respect them still; but we don't fear them.'

While Australia were missing a number of key figures from the previous Ashes series in England, the home nation found that it was also without one particularly significant player. There are no fairytale endings in sport, said Steve Waugh, gimlet-eyed, hard-boiled and unsentimental to the end. Were that he was wrong about that, as the best England captain of the modern era, Michael Vaughan, retired from professional cricket but not from life as of today, will no doubt be thinking.

Vaughan desperately wanted to go out with the crowds cheering and the Ashes again in safe keeping, especially since the manner of his departure from the England captaincy still rankles. Instead, his final innings was at Leicester in Twenty20 cricket, a form of the game that ill-suited his orthodox and graceful style and his wonky knee.

Vaughan's hopes for a fitting final act were encouraged by the selectors, who granted him a central contract last September. That decision can now be seen as either hopelessly deluded or as the gift of a bunch of sentimentalists happy to splurge other people's money. Either way, it was not a good one.

But if the decision to prolong Vaughan's involvement can now be seen for what it was, then Vaughan himself should be spared from criticism because the timing and manner of a player's departure are for him and him alone, and self-delusion is a central requirement for all top-class sportsmen. Bad form, injuries, fatigue and staleness can all be banished when body and mind are willing. The greatest can conjure this trick longer than the rest, but even they must ultimately bow to the inevitable.

It has been clear for a while that Vaughan has been kidding himself – if not the rest of us – since a cruel knee injury curtailed a tour to Pakistan just months after his greatest triumph. Since then he has fought a losing battle with his body, to the point where it hurt to spend one day in the field, never mind five. If his body has betrayed him, so has form, to the extent that his place in the Yorkshire team is no longer a given. Best to go before someone suggests a run-out in the stiffs.

It was an ill-fitting end, then, but only because for the most part he wore the garments so well. For two periods, in 2002–03 as a batsman and 2004–05 as a captain, they were garments lined with ermine, so regal was he at the crease and at the helm of English cricket. Ever since then he has battled to recreate those moments, but, in failure, it should be recognised that few climb such lofty peaks at all.

Only Brian Lara and Sachin Tendulkar in the recent past have pummelled Australia's bowlers into submission as Vaughan did on that 2002–03 tour, when he scored three centuries and 633 runs. His batting was tinged with greatness, pulling Glenn McGrath off his length and driving the rest with rare purity. The worried technician of his youth had been replaced with a more carefree maturity, which is not often the case.

He was not a great player, though, rather a good player who had a great series. The period either side of that purple patch was characterised by constant tinkering with his technique, first to become the player he did and then to try to rediscover that magic. His final average of 41.44, with 18 Test hundreds, reflects that of a very good, not great, Test player.

It is his captaincy, both in the build-up to 2005 and during that dramatic series, for which Vaughan will be remembered. His leadership combined the best of Lancashire, where he was born, and of Yorkshire, where he was raised. His outward calm and sense of enjoyment (the Lancastrian in him) enabled a talented bunch of cricketers express themselves fully and so reach their potential, and his ruthlessness and self-awareness (the Yorkshire side) gave him the necessary distance and authority.

As the rest of the country bit their nails to the quick during that unforgettable summer, Vaughan was privately sick with worry, but he never let the stress show and always exuded an air of utter confidence. He was at the height of his powers in that series, but he enjoyed more than a one-swallow summer. He led England to 26 wins, six more than Peter May, and must rank alongside May as England's finest post-war captain.

There is much to be grateful for despite the messy ending. He goes with our thanks for some memorable moments and with the hope of continued fulfilment beyond the boundary.

The day before the opening Test of the 1995 series, Mark Taylor, the captain of Australia, was asked a simple question: 'How many Englishmen would get into the Australian team?' His answer was equally straightforward: 'None,' he said, although he conceded that Darren Gough's ebullience and general good humour would make him a decent twelfth man.

Before the 2005 series, Ricky Ponting, in a rare show of Australian humility, admitted that Andrew Flintoff might just sneak into the Australian XI; and Flintoff and Kevin Pietersen would have been certainties in any composite team before the 2006–07 white-wash. For the most part, though, the last two decades have been about individual mismatches. Which spinner would you rather have faced in 2003: Shane Warne or Richard Dawson?

Matching up the relative merits of the individuals in each team is just about the roughest calculation of where the balance of power lies. But why spend hours crafting a decent column when you can get away with this? It takes no account of what might be called a team's 'corporate' spirit, of captaincy or of luck. Will Pietersen trip up (over his ego, perhaps) as Glenn McGrath did before Edgbaston in 2005, and so deprive England of their best player?

Nevertheless, if a team is outgunned, man to man, in every department, it has little chance of success. I've looked at the two teams that each may like to put out onto the park (for example, I've assumed that Shane Watson will be fit). How do the Ashes class of 2009 stack up?

Andrew Strauss v Phillip Hughes:

The general consensus is that England's self-interested counties have stymied the national team by allowing Hughes a stint in England prior to the Ashes. I don't go along with that. Strauss has had time to have a good look at the left-hander's unorthodox technique, while Hughes's brilliance in the early part of the season has raised expectations to an almost unmatchable level. But he will find England's attack a far tougher proposition than Second Division bowlers.

It may be that he is another genius from the Outback, the next in a long lineage that has included Don Bradman, Stan McCabe, Dougie Walters and Michael Slater, but we cannot yet be sure. He may carry all before him or he may simply fall flat on his face. Strauss, meanwhile, is proven, dependable and tough, and in the last 12 months has been in the form of his life. On whom would *you* put your hard-earned?

Verdict: Strauss.

Alastair Cook v Simon Katich:

Cook, fine young player that he is, has not yet taken his game
to the next level. He is much tougher than his choirboy looks
suggest, but is always battling his technique, which has more
holes than a Swiss cheese. Australia will look to starve him of
bread-and-butter leg-side runs and the short ball, and make him
drive through the off side – a tactic that rendered him shot-less
at times in the last Ashes series.

Katich was vulnerable to the swinging ball during the 2005
Ashes series and has a modest record against England. Since
2005, though, he has risen to the challenge by carrying all before
him in Australian domestic cricket and forcing the selectors'
hand when many thought his time had gone. If England get
sucked into bowling too straight as he shuffles across his stumps,
he could have a profitable time.

Verdict: Katich.

Ricky Ponting v Ravi Bopara:

The champion and the challenger. Both these players are at
opposite ends of the career spectrum, Ponting having achieved
everything in the game, Bopara setting out to do just that.
Bopara looked a potential champion against West Indies, but
how much of a test was that? And questions remain: he was
dropped on numerous occasions and Shane Warne has clearly
seen something in his temperament that would have got the
great spinner twitching his fingers and loosening his vocal
chords. Ponting, meanwhile, looks as hungry as ever, even if he

is getting to the stage in life where other things – principally family – may start to take the edge off his game.

Verdict: Ponting.

Kevin Pietersen v Michael Clarke:

I expect Pietersen to rise to the occasion and cement his position as one of the great batsmen of the moment. Like all captains, Ponting hates the feeling of not being in control of events in the field, and Pietersen is the player who can change the course of a game in a session. Clarke, though, has questions to answer: he has never been that successful in England, either for Hampshire as an overseas player, or in the 2005 series and technically he has looked suspect against the moving ball.

Verdict: Pietersen.

Paul Collingwood v Michael Hussey:

Collingwood always seems as though he has got something to prove and his great strength over the years has been the way he has responded to that pressure. But so far he has had an anonymous season, and his performance in the World Twenty20 did little for his reputation or confidence. Hussey, after a magnificent start to his career, is finding things tougher now. A combination of greater awareness of his strengths and weaknesses and life on the road has taken the edge off his game. Collingwood may be tougher; Hussey, on song, is the better player.

Verdict: Hussey.

Andrew Flintoff v Shane Watson:

Do we need to go on?
   Verdict: Flintoff.

Matt Prior v Brad Haddin:

Tough one. Prior is probably the better batsman – he could get in England's team as a batsman alone – although Haddin, while no Adam Gilchrist, is no slouch with the stick. And 'keeping? Haddin is no Ian Healy either, but he is tidier than Prior. Prior has improved and kept well in the West Indies series, but there is always a fumble around the corner which will attract the critics' attention.
   Verdict: draw.

Stuart Broad v Mitchell Johnson:

Two outstanding young cricketers. Johnson has come of age in the last 12 months, leading Australia's attack with menace and skill, and becoming a dangerous batsman down the order. He will be the bowler who will cause Pietersen, and England's other batsmen, most problems. Broad has considerable talent of his own, having increased his pace this year, but he doesn't yet have Johnson's explosiveness or ability to turn a game with ball or bat.
   Verdict: Johnson.

James Anderson v Brett Lee:

The girls might have a battle on their hands deciding who they would prefer on their arm, but, right now, each captain would rather Anderson was taking the new ball. Lee has the reputation, greater pedigree and more Test wickets (310 to Anderson's 128), but while his career graph is past its peak and now declining, Anderson's is on the rise. Lee has never really enjoyed bowling in England (average 45.44 as against 30.81 overall) where his low trajectory means a lack of bounce, nor has he been at his best against England (average 40.61). Anderson is at the peak of his powers, able to swing the ball both ways at good pace and strong enough to bowl fast all day and stay fit throughout the series.

Verdict: Anderson.

Graeme Swann v Nathan Hauritz:

Hauritz may not play if Australia decide to put all their eggs in the pace bowling basket, and their uncertainty over whether to play their one specialist spinner, or leave the spin bowling to part-timers like Clarke, Katich and Marcus North, tells you all you need to know about Hauritz. There are no bad Australian Test cricketers, but it is hard to see Hauritz giving England's batsmen sleepless nights. Graeme Swann continues to surprise with his clever variations of flight and spin, and with his evident relish for the heat of battle. Hauritz spends more time bemoaning his bad luck at following Shane Warne. Boo hoo.

Verdict: Swann.

Ryan Sidebottom v Peter Siddle:

Will it be Sidebottom or Graham Onions or Stephen Harmison? Will it be Siddle or Stuart Clark or Ben Hilfenhaus? Sidebottom–Siddle is the battle of the hot-headed red-heads.

Siddle is a relative unknown here but is better than his obscurity might suggest. Wholehearted in the best traditions of Australian fast bowling, his last ball of the day will be as heavy as his first and his tongue is sure to be given plenty of use. He has a good record in his brief career to date. Sidebottom has a temper, too, although it is not always best utilised. He has the advantage of his left-arm angle and swing, but carries question marks about his fitness and ability to bowl quickly for prolonged periods.

Verdict: draw.

A composite team, then, includes five Englishmen, four Australians and two hybrids – Haddin/Prior, Sidebottom/Siddle – the last being a truly terrifying thought. For the first time in over two decades England shade it on pure ability. The heart, and the head, says England – just.

2

First Test, Cardiff

8–12 July

The realisation of an ambition should always be acknowledged, and so Glamorgan can be rightly proud of the ground they have produced and of becoming the 100th Test match venue. A lack of ambition, though, should always be highlighted and condemned, and the ECB can take no credit for staging the opening Ashes Test at a stadium that can hold only 16,000 spectators.

They are touchy about this criticism in these parts, since it is perceived as some kind of anti-Welsh bias. It is nothing of the kind. It is a criticism of the ECB's policy of awarding Test matches according to the size of a county's wallet, rather than the quality of its cricket facilities, and, more importantly, a criticism of the decision to spread international cricket thinly among grounds with minuscule seating capacity.

Of Australia's five Ashes venues, only Perth has a smaller capacity, at about 22,000, than England's biggest, Lord's, at 30,000. Australia's five major grounds give a capacity of around 93 seats per 1000 population in an international summer, as opposed to England's approximately 21 seats per 1000 population.

The result, inevitably, is much higher ticket prices in England. At Cardiff, tickets range from £40–£90; they are higher at Lord's, of course, where only 60 per cent of seating is available to the general public. Instead of more international grounds, surely there should be fewer with bigger capacities. More games at high-capacity grounds would, in turn, result in lower ticket prices. Cricket's lack of affordability means it is, increasingly, targeting an affluent minority.

There are other, cricketing, reasons why it would have been preferable not to have staged the opening game at what is, for England, virtually a neutral ground. But the decision to award the opening Test match to Cardiff was taken not by the Major Match Group, whose decision it was to award the Test to Cardiff, but by the previous England management headed by Peter Moores and Michael Vaughan. It was a case of anywhere but Lord's, where England have not won a Test against Australia since 1934.

Despite the caution shown in the selection of the venue, it is a measure of England's progress under Andrew Strauss and Andy Flower that the thirteen names revealed for the first Test contained no surprises. Before England departed for the Caribbean earlier in the year, after the convulsions that saw the bitter departure of Kevin Pietersen and Peter Moores as captain and head coach respectively, the consensus was that such instability six months before the Ashes was disastrous.

In fact, it was necessary. England had backed the wrong captain and the wrong coach – to complete a miserable year for those making decisions on behalf of English cricket – better, therefore, to get rid of the weeds before the garden became unmanageable. Since then a mixture of common sense and tough love has resulted in a situation where ten of the team pick themselves on merit and recent record, rather than reputation or promise.

The selectors had only two decisions to make during a week in which they split their time and energies between Edgbaston, Worcester and Cardiff, to which Geoff Miller made periodic visits to watch the development of a pitch that has had an unhealthy amount of speculation over its likely properties. It will be 22 yards, like any other, and, as is always the case, the better team will come out on top.

Two decisions, then, which concerned the identity of the fourth seamer and the second spinner. In both cases, the selectors made the right call sticking with, in Graham Onions, the man in possession and, with Monty Panesar, the tried and tested. Whoever gets the final nod will depend entirely on conditions, with Ian Bell a non-starter unless food poisoning or swine flu strikes.

Stephen Harmison made a late push for inclusion with two outstanding new-ball spells during the Lions' match at Worcester, when he made Phillip Hughes look not so much genius as novice and the temptation to include him must have been strong. But Harmison, 30, looked weary as the game progressed (mind you, a few others did, too) and his days of playing consecutive Test matches are at an end. It is a case now, with Harmison, of using and discarding wherever necessary (and, please, no central contract whatever happens over the next two months) and whenever conditions dictate. Given that Cardiff is likely to be slow, better to keep him fresh for Lord's, if fresh impetus is needed then.

Ryan Sidebottom remains in the queue, but has not done enough yet since his return to full fitness. Besides, Onions has done nothing wrong. He was outstanding in the early-season Test matches, before the World Twenty20 banished those to the back of our minds, and remains the country's leading wicket-taker and most prolific taker of five-wicket hauls. From close to the stumps, he will bowl well at Australia's phalanx of left-handers and, at 26, is younger, fitter and hungrier than Harmison. If Hughes needs his rib-cage tickling, then in any case Andrew Flintoff is quicker and more accurate than Harmison.

Seasonal statistics suggest the talk of Cardiff being a spinner's paradise has been overplayed, but if England do pick two spinners then it will be because they expect them to be impact bowlers. Adil Rashid's all-round capabilities, therefore, are a red herring. He can bat and field better than Panesar, but at the moment he cannot bowl as well. Strauss needed to ask himself one simple question when comparing the merits of the two: come the fifth day, with Australia needing 250 to win and the ball turning, who would he have more faith in as a bowler? Panesar is that man.

And what of the Australians? In the absence of Shane Watson, who seems to have the perfect body for the beach but not the cricket pitch, they have one decision to make. Should they play Nathan Hauritz? The off-spinner found some turn on the final day in Worcester, but that might have come too late for his chances. In all but the dustiest conditions, they can be expected to play four seamers, with reverse swing from Brett Lee and Stuart Clark's metronomic accuracy providing the cutting edge and pressure that came from the old ball in one man's hands previously.

Hauritz has little of Shane Warne's ability, which he can do nothing about, but none of his presence at the crease, either, which he can. A word here, a pause there, a knowing look, all gave the impression that the batsman was dancing to Warne's tune, but there is none of that with Hauritz.

It is the lack of aura generally that stood out watching Australia go about their business in Worcester. They have always been among the most down-to-earth, likeable and approachable of cricketers off the field. It was good to see some of them walking back to their hotel from the New Road ground last week carrying their backpacks and not a security guard in sight, for instance – something from which England's more starry-eyed and precious bunch could learn.

But along with that bloke-next-door image there has always been, in the last decade, a heavy sprinkling of cricketing stardust. Sit a table away from Warne and McGrath at breakfast, and you know that there were two players with more than a thousand Test wickets munching through their toast; or if you happened to be next to Justin Langer and Matthew Hayden there were 53 Test centuries staring back at you. It takes the edge off their approachability.

That aura, that presence, is just not there now – indeed, there are a few who could easily walk down any high street in England and not be recognised. England, then, walk on to the field at Cardiff as equals, in their own minds and everyone else's. That is a big change.

Australia are a workmanlike side: fit, professional, battle-hardened, as all Australian cricketers are, but workmanlike nonetheless. It is a team typified, perhaps, by the likes of Marcus

North, Simon Katich, Brad Haddin and Peter Siddle, good cricketers all but none of whom would have made any Australia team between 1993 and 2001 and all of whom have yet to prove their Ashes mettle.

Ashes history points to Australia – even in England where they have won more Tests than the home side. But the make-up of these teams suggests one of the tightest series since Reginald Brooks, with his satirical newspaper notice, and a love story between Ivo Bligh and an Aussie girl from the outback, gave rise to the greatest sporting rivalry of them all. Maybe, in the end, it will all come down to that bane of the professional sportsman's life: the great uncontrollables – an umpiring decision here, a bad bounce there.

Whatever the outcome, though, another great narrative, full of great characters, great deeds and great drama, is about to unfold. Preceded by Twenty20 cricket and followed by seven one-day internationals, it is an Ashes series that can make a statement for the form of the game that will test these cricketers – mentally, technically and physically – as no other cricket can.

I'm sure that the same emotion is being experienced by the opening batsmen on the two sides. Only a few dozen people know how two of Simon Katich, Phillip Hughes, Andrew Strauss and Alastair Cook will be feeling just before 11 o'clock on Wednesday morning, when the talking finally stops and the action starts. The called-upon pair will be not so much opening batsmen as postmen, delivering to the audience a message that will reveal much about the state of mind and readiness of their respective teams. Some responsibility.

Those opening moments have taken on greater significance ever since the 1994–95 series, when an impish Michael Slater slotted the first ball of the series through cover point for four to signal another period of Australian dominance. In 2005, Stephen Harmison's menace and the unconcerned reaction of England's fielders when he drew first blood – literally – from Australia said much about England's uncompromising attitude, while the ball that ended up in second slip's hands eighteen months later suggested they were still suffering a hangover from their previous heroics.

It's the quiet of those opening seconds that gets you – unique, in my experience, to Ashes series. The bowler thundering in and the crowd utterly engrossed, more than a hundred years of gripping narrative distilled into one silent moment as expectation, promise and, it must be said, a fair dollop of hot air gives way to the next chapter in the story. In the dressing room, all the hopes and fears of the team are carried by the openers, alone in the middle with just their techniques and mental strength for company.

Katich, back in the Australian team after a stunning revival in domestic cricket following his disappointing 2005 campaign, has already given consideration to that moment. 'Even though we're still some way out, I've given a lot of thought to those opening sequences, especially since I haven't opened in an Ashes series before. On the day I'll go through my usual routines. I'll already have gone through the tapes and worked out what to

The teams line up as if to greet royalty for the ceremonies at the start of the first npower Test in Cardiff, which became the 100th Test match venue.

Kevin Pietersen has to stretch to reach Nathan Hauritz's delivery and top-edged his sweep into the hands of Simon Katich at short leg. His score of 69 was England's highest in their first innings total of 435.

Graeme Swann hits out on the morning of the second day when England's tail added 99 runs at six an over to leave Australia's attack looking ragged.

Simon Katich completed a superb undefeated century on the second day, as Australia made hefty inroads into England's score.

Ricky Ponting's fury at getting out to Monty Panesar, having made 150, showed that he wanted to make an even more emphatic statement about his intentions to retain the Ashes.

Brad Haddin launches one to the leg-side boundary off Graeme Swann during his innings of 121. Together with Marcus North, he added 200 for the sixth wicket to help Australia to declare on 674 for 6, their highest score in the Ashes for 75 years.

Alastair Cook falls early in the second innings to Mitchell Johnson to get England off to the worst possible start.

Paul Collingwood cannot believe what he's done after giving a catch to Michael Hussey in the gully after almost six hours of gritty resistance.

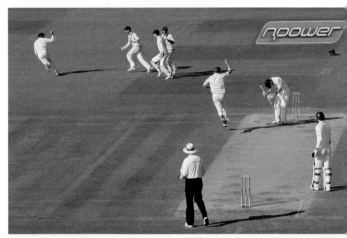

Now it was down to Collingwood's 'batting buddy', Monty Panesar, and Jimmy Anderson to hold out for the last 69 balls to help England escape with a draw.

Andrew Flintoff's oddly timed announcement of his Test retirement came the day before the Lord's Test and ensured that he remained the focus of attention throughout the match. He responded in inimitable fashion.

Huge numbers of MCC members queued for hours to ensure they could get the best seats for the eagerly anticipated second npower Test.

Andrew Strauss was in imperious form on the first day at Lord's, finishing on 161 not out to help England to a strong position.

Ricky Ponting has some words of advice for his strike bowler, Mitchell Johnson, who had a match to forget at Lord's.

James Anderson is already appealing for LBW against Ricky Ponting, with the ball still in the air on its way to Andrew Strauss. However, umpire Rudi Koertzen gave him out caught.

Kevin Pietersen, who looked to be struggling for fitness throughout the Test, made an uncharacteristically slow 44 in the second innings. After the match, he had an operation on his Achilles' tendon that put him out of the rest of the series.

Phillip Hughes is controversially given out as this catch by Andrew Strauss was not referred to the third umpire. For him, too, it would be his last innings of the series, as he was dropped for Shane Watson.

Michael Clarke is congratulated by Brad Haddin on reaching his century towards the end of the fourth day. The pair batted almost 50 overs to set up a highly improbable chance of victory on the last day.

But the chance of an Australian victory disappeared when Clarke charged down the wicket and missed one from Graeme Swann.

Andrew Flintoff celebrates after bowling out Peter Siddle to complete his second Ashes five-wicket haul, which earned him the Man of the Match award.

expect, so I'll have a few hits and then make sure that I make half an hour for myself to just sit quietly and contemplate.'

Katich seems like the unassuming type, but he is a man of contradictions: the son of a wine grower with no sense of smell, and the quiet man with a volcanic temper. Few remember that at Trent Bridge, when Ricky Ponting's cool melted having been run out by Gary Pratt, Katich was fined for a remarkable outburst of his own after a poor leg-before decision; and when, in February, Michael Clarke wanted to leave the Australian dressing room after a victory before the team song had been sung, it was Katich who grabbed him by the throat.

'I keep my temper under control most of the time, but my competitiveness is one of my strengths, and it's one of the reasons why I've played longer than some thought I might at first-class level. As for the incident with Michael, that's over with and we've both moved on, but it showed how much the traditions of the baggy green mean to me. At the start of this tour, we all sat down and talked of what the Ashes means to us, and our earliest Ashes memories [Katich's being when he was in ninth grade at school of Terry Alderman tormenting Graham Gooch in the 1989 series] and it was clear to me, after that, that this tour and the Ashes remain the pinnacle for Australian players.

'I know we've been written off in some quarters, but we're very comfortable in our skin at the moment. The South African tour [which Australia won 2-1 recently] was central to that. Without being disrespectful to the older guys – because they were all champions and their records speak for themselves – once the selectors brought in some younger players that had a huge impact on us. They energised us and I think Ricky [Ponting] has been excited by the chance to shape a new team and some new careers, people like [Peter] Siddle and [Mitchell] Johnson. He's as committed as I've ever seen him.'

Since Katich has finished on the winning side against England only once, he is also that rare breed of Australian cricketer whose Ashes experiences have been mainly disappointing and losing ones. In 2005, England's swing bowling quartet tormented him outside off stump with close-set off-side fields, packing an arc between slip and backward point, so that he finished the series bereft of confidence and, shortly afterwards, out of the team.

'Having experienced 2005, they will probably come at me with the same plans, but I'm a much better player now. I'm very proud of the work that I've put in to get back into the team. I did a lot of work with Bobby Simpson, mainly on my balance, so that shots which were squirting square, or behind square on the off side in 2005, I'm now hitting a lot straighter. In 2005, because the ball wasn't going where I wanted it to, my confidence went and I began to go into my shell. I'll be much more assertive this time around.'

Katich looked as good as his word against England Lions at Worcester, where he scored 95 in the first innings and got another start in the second. But what about his opening partner, Phillip Hughes, who was given such a working over by Harmison? 'He'll be fine. He's got a great temperament and for a young player he knows his game really well. He's such a cheeky fella, plays with a smile on his face and relishes the contest.

'Generally, our preparation has been a lot better this time

around. Reverse swing caught us off guard in 2005. This time we've worked hard on that aspect of our game, the bowlers working with Troy Cooley to swing the old ball much earlier than before, and the batsmen getting bowlers to scuff up old balls in the nets so that we can practice against it. We won't be caught off guard like that again.'

Indeed, a reluctance to be caught out also pervaded the press conference before the Cardiff Test. Nobody seemed prepared to say it, least of all two captains who are too long in the tooth and canny to be drawn into silly predictions, but the feeling around Test cricket's 100th venue seemed unmistakable: England, with a more incisive and a more varied bowling attack, have not had a better chance in two decades of beginning an Ashes series with a victory.

The last time that happened was in 1997 at Edgbaston, but the disparity in ability between the two teams then was such that any English advantage was swiftly overturned. But times change, as has, more pertinently, the Australian team, and England will walk out in Cardiff this morning confident not only that they can match Australia man for man, but also, in Andrew Flintoff and Kevin Pietersen, that they possess game-changing players of their own.

Ricky Ponting spoke movingly about what the Ashes mean to him and about how, when his uncle, Greg Campbell, was selected for the 1989 series in England, Ponting went down to his house just to look at and touch Campbell's Australian kit for that tour. Australian cricket still does symbolism and meaning much better than England.

There is no doubt that the Australia captain remains deeply and impressively committed to the cause, even if he will do well to match the messianic fervour with which he went about his business in 2006–07. But no amount of symbolism or rhetoric can hide the fact that this is a good rather than great Australian team and that, so close to the start of the series, question marks about their constituent parts remain.

Squally showers meant that the pitch was under lock and key before Ponting spoke to the media and so, blind to the surface, he had no option but to say that all options (with the exception of Brett Lee and Shane Watson) remain open. However, in Lee's absence, uncertainties abound: do they play Nathan Hauritz, who gives the impression that he doesn't think he should be here; Ben Hilfenhaus, who did so well in South Africa but struggled at Hove; or Andrew McDonald, the all-rounder who has yet to don his match gear on tour?

None has Lee's star quality, his experience of Ashes contests or his match-winning potential, even though it is unlikely that reverse swing, which plays such a big part in his armoury, will be much in evidence at the SWALEC Stadium. The pitch is an unknown quantity for these players but it does not feel hard, or abrasive, and with the outfield lush and verdant, the bowlers will look to orthodox swing and spin as their main allies this week.

This should suit England. Like Ponting, Andrew Strauss was keeping his cards close to his chest, but this was out of desire rather than any uncertainty. The England captain said that he knew his own mind and, despite the weather and the short, straight boundaries that would give the most confident spinner nightmares, he intimated strongly that Monty Panesar would play in a classically balanced five-man attack. This has certainly been the plan from some way out, ever since the Trinidad Test last winter, when Panesar played Ernie Wise to Graeme Swann's Eric Morecambe.

When asked about Panesar, Strauss gave a powerful endorsement of the one player in his squad to have really struggled for form this summer. 'Panesar is a very good Test match bowler, as he has proved time and again, even though he has not had a great season so far. There is something about being back in the England fold that turns a light on for him. He's got his unique role in the dressing room and he feels comfortable in the environment. He's bowled well in the nets, accurately with good bounce and spin, and I think this game will bring out the best in him.'

Barring a last-minute change of plan, or a day of rain, two spinners it will be to complement James Anderson's swing, Stuart Broad's line and Flintoff's pace: as good and as balanced an attack as England have put out in recent years. Ponting, then, will look to England's batting line-up as the point of weakness, hoping that Ravi Bopara blanches on the biggest stage, that Paul Collingwood's technique is undermined and that Matt Prior is one too high in the order at number six.

Like bullion in a recession, Australia's middle order of Mike Hussey, Michael Clarke and Ponting is a safe haven in times of trouble. Phillip Hughes and Simon Katich, though, represent a riskier investment. Hughes must now show the mental strength to quell the doubts that abound after his working-over at Worcester against England Lions, otherwise the decision to pick only one specialist opener will be exposed, while Katich's returns against England are modest.

Strauss said that his team are ready and well prepared and 'champing at the bit' for the action to start. He expressed confidence that he had the personnel for the battles to come: 'All eleven are in good form and are looking very confident to me. I like the characters in my team. They will not be easily overawed and they will back themselves. I can feel a great deal of excitement around, which is better than nerves or tension. They look relaxed and confident in practice and I've got a lot of faith in them to deliver when the time comes.'

When asked to reveal his final message to his team, he declined, saying that he had a couple of thoughts that he wanted to get across but that, with emotions running high enough already, it would not be a time for 'Churchillian' speeches.

There is, though, one simple message that he could get across: he could look Alastair Cook, Pietersen, Collingwood, Flintoff, Anderson and Panesar squarely in the eye and ask them whether they remembered how they felt on that beautiful but bleak day in Sydney two-and-a-half years ago. Do they remember wave upon wave of Australian triumphalism crashing over them? Do they remember the humiliation they felt on becoming part of only the second England team to be whitewashed on Australian soil? Well do they?

Day 1, Wednesday 8 July

Close of play: England 336 for 7

It was with all manner of pomp and ceremony that Test cricket came to Cardiff. With the Welsh Royal Guards, feted opera singers and an equally splendid red carpet greeting the players before the start of the day, it was as if we were witnessing a royal occasion not a cricket match. The cricket itself was not exactly of the blue-blooded variety – there were too many unforced errors for that – but it was, as you would expect on the opening day of an Ashes series, red-blooded; England finishing an intriguing first day on 336 for 7.

Whether this represents a good return or a missed opportunity, only time will tell, but the suspicion is that the home team will be happy with their day's work, especially given their habit of starting Ashes series more slowly than a four-mile steeplechaser. Australia would be content to have taken seven wickets having lost the toss, but this pitch has already shown signs of taking spin, England have five bowlers to Australia's four, two spinners to their one, and Australia must bat last. There was also consistent swing for Ben Hilfenhaus throughout the day, which will interest James Anderson when his turn comes.

After a sticky morning when three wickets were lost through a mixture of nerves, poor shot selection and Mitchell Johnson, there were half-centuries for Kevin Pietersen, Paul Collingwood and Matt Prior, whose blade sounded the sweetest of all, and a pleasing cameo from Andrew Flintoff, who seems determined to try to recreate the mood of 2005 and the freedom with which he

61

batted in that series. Nobody, though, could go on and dominate the day, and convert a start into an innings of real substance, so the lasting impression is one of an opportunity missed.

For Australia it was a mixed day. After a bright morning, they went wicket-less in the afternoon, when it was clear that Ricky Ponting, setting some defensive fields, has learnt to cut his cloth according to the bowlers at his disposal. Then, when the touring team's captain took the second new ball after tea, they leaked runs at an alarming rate before Peter Siddle struck twice late in the day to redress the balance.

At least Ponting got his selections spot on, Nathan Hauritz, the spinner, generally holding his own before taking the key wicket of Pietersen and Hilfenhaus bowling steadily. There were signs, too, that Johnson had started to find his rhythm, picking up Ravi Bopara and Andrew Strauss, the former with a magnificently disguised slower ball, the second with a rapid bouncer that Strauss punched to slip.

For a while in the afternoon, as the cricket turned attritional, it looked as if English cricket's version of royalty, Pietersen, might treat his subjects to a century as he often does on these showpiece occasions. He was not at his vintage best, to be sure, showing unusual nerves at the start of his innings as Australia looked to exploit his penchant for playing across full, straight deliveries with a high back-lift, but when he survived a plumb-looking leg-before on 61 and a dropped catch by Michael Clarke at extra cover on 66, it felt as if it might be his day.

Ironically, it was Hauritz, the man that most thought would be a lamb to Pietersen's slaughter, who cut short his stay.

Pietersen had been forced to play a patient hand by Ponting's deep set fields – what John Buchanan, the former Australia coach, would have called playing on the Pietersen ego – and he managed to pierce the boundary ropes only three times in his first fifty runs. His bread-and-butter stroke off Hauritz had been the wristy paddle around the corner for a single a time and trying that stroke again brought his downfall.

Eyeing Pietersen's premeditated sweep, Hauritz pushed the ball wider. So wide, in fact, that had the batsman essayed a square cut he might have struggled to reach it. Instead, he attempted to manoeuvre the ball behind square on the leg side, but succeeded only in top-edging it onto his helmet, short-leg taking the offering. Depending on your take on these things, Pietersen, again, will be hero or villain. Poor shot selection will suffice.

Pietersen had enjoyed another three-figure collaboration with Paul Collingwood, their eighth together in what is now the most successful fourth-wicket partnership that England have produced. Collingwood is the artisan to Pietersen's royalty and is always happy to sail along in his slipstream, a fact acknowledged by Ponting, who was happy to allow the Durham man the lion's share of the strike. It needed a top-class snare by Brad Haddin, moving more sharply to his right than he had in the warm-up matches, to end Collingwood's stay once Hilfenhaus had located the outside edge.

At 241 for 5, with the new ball just ten overs away, it was the second time in the day that Australia had sniffed an opportunity and, at times, it needed thrilling strokeplay from Prior and Flintoff to give England renewed momentum. Prior's cockiness was impressive given that this is his first Ashes Test, and he was severe on anything with the merest hint of width. His confidence seemed to rub off on Flintoff, who played in the manner of a man with a point to prove. Both were bowled courtesy of inside edges and the persevering Siddle.

Prior and Flintoff finished the day as Bopara had started it, once Alastair Cook had departed to Mike Hussey's spring-heeled catch in the gully. But whereas Prior and Flintoff's aggression was a deliberate counter-attack to neuter a dangerous situation, the suspicion remains that Bopara's curious innings reflected the nerves in the team generally.

He was given a typically Antipodean greeting by Siddle, who thundered a second-ball bouncer into his neck: welcome to Ashes cricket, cobber. Clearly unsettled, he got off the mark eight balls later with a streaky inside-edged four to fine leg before driving airily on a number of occasions. It was noticeable how much of the stumps the bowlers could see and how far away from his body Bopara was defending the ball, technical blemishes that will keep Australia's bowlers interested. Was it nerves or an iffy technique? England will hope the former.

Day 2, Thursday 9 July

Close of play: England 435; Australia 249 for 1

There was a time just after lunch yesterday when English cricket was transported back to 2005. Andrew Flintoff was bearing down upon the crease, releasing thunderbolt after thunderbolt, seemingly unchanged over the four-year period even though much water has flowed under the pedalo since then. The crowd was alive to the possibilities, chanting its hero's name ball after ball, and Australia were under the hammer.

It proved to be illusory, nothing more than a fleeting remembrance of a time that Ricky Ponting, for one, has no intention of embracing again. It was that painful memory that galvanised Ponting's team to the whitewash in 2006–07, and, to judge from the flawless way the Australia captain played yesterday, it is a memory that continues to haunt him and drive him forward.

Ponting scored a hundred of the crispest runs imaginable and shared an unbroken 189-run partnership with Simon Katich, who scored a century of his own and whose game is much improved from the unreliable model of 2005. A day that began badly for Australia ended in the best possible fashion, Katich celebrating his first Ashes hundred three overs before the close, and Ponting scampering through to his eighth, and, staggeringly, his 38th in Test cricket, during the final over of the day.

Australia are not yet in a commanding position, trailing as they do by 186, but they bat deep and, if the example of Ponting and Katich is followed, they will bat long: a nod in the direction of England's batsmen, perhaps, who were so profligate on the first day. England will rue the absence of swing for James Anderson, the ineffectiveness of Graeme Swann and Monty Panesar, and Stuart Broad's niggling calf injury, which prevented him from bowling for most of the final session.

Ponting arrived at the crease after a flighty innings from Phillip Hughes that can have done little for the captain's nerves. In truth, England bowled poorly at Hughes, giving him too much width and concentrating, to the exclusion of everything else, on the short ball. Accordingly, this jack-in-a-box batsman got off to a flier, dispatching Broad to the off-side fence three times and putting any doubts that emerged after his working over at Worcester firmly to the back of his mind.

But not once did he give he give the impression of permanence. Indeed, it is hard to think of a more unorthodox opening batsman who has played regularly and successfully at the highest level, and when Flintoff removed his sweater straight after lunch, Hughes's stay seemed destined to be short-lived. Giving himself room to hit through point once too often, Flintoff located Hughes's inside edge and Matt Prior accepted the offering, diving to his right.

All the attention at the start of this tour was on Hughes, which probably suited the unassuming Katich just fine. He was happy for the anonymity at the start of his innings yesterday, too, as England's bowlers lavished their attention on the younger man.

Later, Katich had to defer to Ponting, when the Tasmanian became only the fourth man in history to pass 11,000 Test runs. Ponting passed that landmark with his 40th run, joining an elite group comprising Sachin Tendulkar, Brian Lara and Allan Border, and the way in which he acknowledged it, with just a cursory wave of the bat to the Australia balcony, was the clearest possible indicator that he is not playing this series simply to fatten his own statistics. Statistically, though, since Ponting has the highest average of the four, his place at cricket's top table is assured.

Quiet and unassuming Katich may be, but for England's bowlers yesterday, he was deadly efficient. He gave one chance, on ten, when Flintoff could not hold onto a sharp return catch, but barely lofted the ball above the turf thereafter. Limited, in some ways, he restricted himself to drives, tucks off his hip and the odd late cut, but it was the way he neutered the threat of Panesar and Swann, who bowled 31 wicketless overs between them, that was the foundation of his success. He played them superbly, his judgement of length outstanding.

Swann will find life tougher than he did against the West Indies left-handers, although he will argue that Katich ought to have been given out leg-before on 56, and Panesar has clearly not learnt from his failings against Graeme Smith last summer. Like Smith, Katich moved across his stumps and milked the spinner through the leg side but Panesar, as then, countered with little, refusing to chance his arm from round the wicket. There is time yet for England's spin twins to get into this game, but if they are rendered powerless here, England may be forced to change tack for the rest of the summer.

If that happens, Ponting will feel that England are already dancing to the beat of his drum, as they did for the final four hours of the day. There was something deeply impressive about the way the Australian captain played, meeting virtually every-thing with a giant stride forward and the maker's name never less than fully in view. His driving off the front foot was a treat.

It was an innings all the more impressive for what preceded it, for rarely can an Australian captain have witnessed his first-choice attack being put to the sword by England tail-enders. They played with glorious abandon, rattling along at six an over and reducing Australia to a bit of a rabble.

Chief pain in the backside for Australia was Swann who hit

his opposite number, Nathan Hauritz, for three successive boundaries, the last from a reverse sweep that had Kevin Pietersen purring with pleasure on the balcony. Swann could possibly lay claim to the shot of the innings, too, a marvellous lofted straight drive off Ben Hilfenhaus that landed a nanometre inside the rope at the Taff End.

Swann looked in the mood to go on and on, but was left stranded after Anderson failed to clear mid-on, and Panesar edged to gully to give Hauritz his third wicket. England are employing a 'buddy' system, where a top-order player is given the responsibility of improving the batting of a designated tail-ender. Paul Collingwood is the unfortunate minder for Panesar, who was the only England player not to make double figures. Poor Colly, if he can improve Panesar's batting, he can expect to trade in his MBE for something better.

Day 3, Friday, 10 July

Close of play: England 435; Australia 479 for 5

Is it cowardly to pray for rain? was the title of a delicious book about the Ashes here four years ago, the title reflecting the general hope that, with England ahead, The Oval would be swamped under a deluge. There were mutterings about the weekend forecast at Cardiff yesterday morning, too, the difference being that we are only three days into the series: cowardly, certainly, and far too early to pray for assistance.

England needed to get themselves out of a hole of Australia's and their own making yesterday rather than rely on natural forces outside of their control. On the second evening, Andrew Flintoff reminded the team that they had been in this situation before, at The Oval in 2005 as it happens, but as well-meaning as that advice was, it is time England stopped living in the past. Wickets are scored and runs are taken by taking charge of the here and now.

Instead, England needed to realise that another day of chanceless Australian run-making and it would be themselves batting last on a deteriorating pitch and not Australia, a state of affairs far more likely to galvanise them into action than misty memories of four years ago. Accordingly, they came bouncing out of the gates to the strains of 'Jerusalem', although with Andrew Strauss setting overly defensive fields, especially when the second new ball was taken, the messages were mixed ones. It was an indifferent day full stop for Strauss, three wickets in the morning raising false hopes before Michael Clarke and Marcus North, with a restorative partnership of 143, slammed the door in his team's face.

Then, after rain prevented play for two hours after tea, the players came back to play Test cricket under floodlights for the first time on home soil, and Clarke was promptly dismissed, feathering a glove down the leg side off Stuart Broad.

With heavy clouds lying over Cardiff, rain in the air and movement, at last, off the pitch, Flintoff and Broad ran in urgently, sensing an opportunity, but only six overs were possible before the umpires took the players off again for – wait for it – bad light.

Clarke was particularly impressive during his stay, purring along like a smoothly running motor, severe on anything short, quick to the drive and twinkling down the pitch at every opportunity to England's spinners, once dispatching Monty Panesar into the crowd at long-off. Such was Australia's domination of Graeme Swann and Panesar – just one wicket between them in 55 overs – that Strauss was forced to turn to Paul Collingwood's off-cutters just before tea. It reminded old soaks hereabouts of Don Shepherd, the great Glamorgan bowler who might have enjoyed these conditions.

North is more cumbersome on his feet, a super-tanker to Clarke's speedboat, and less talented, too. He was content to play the spinners from the crease, looking to sweep wherever possible, but he was no less effective for that and he gave off a reassuring solidity when facing the seam bowlers. He will be an important player for Australia this summer if he remains in good form and can expect to play a supporting role in England's second innings to Nathan Hauritz, now looming – am I really writing this? – as a threat.

England have been made to work hard for every Australian wicket, which is, of course, exactly how it should be in Test cricket, something the home side's bowlers could mention during the next team meeting. Not that Australia have been defensive, the runs coming at an even three-and-a-half an over throughout the innings.

At the outset, in the nine overs before the new ball became available, the flow of the game resumed firmly in Australia's direction, 32 runs coming without a sniff of a chance. Five times the ball went to the ropes, mostly off England's spin twins who erred too often in line, length and direction. When Ricky Ponting hit yet another Swann full toss down the ground, the thought occurred that maybe the pre-match attention had focused on the wrong off spinner.

The new ball came and the new ball went, twice to the boundary in James Anderson's first over, as Ponting executed textbook illustrations of how to drive and pull. But then things changed quickly, as things tend to do in Test cricket. In the slightly warmer air than the day before, the ball began to respond to Anderson's aching desire, and when the ball swings for Anderson he is a completely different animal, as Simon Katich, too far across to a full inswinger, found to his cost.

Mike Hussey bustled out to the crease like the eager beaver he is, confidence restored after some pre-Test runs against the Lions. Hussey's recent form has mirrored the FTSE index, his last 19 Test matches returning an average of 34.69, as opposed to his first 18, which brought him a Bradmanesque return of 86.18. Was his hundred at Worcester the equivalent of a dead-cat-bounce, or the harbinger of a more permanent recovery? Time will tell, but his stock plummeted a little more yesterday, when Anderson tempted him to drive to a ball that maintained its line rather than swinging in as Hussey expected.

Ponting was up to 150 now, celebrating another milestone curtly, his 13th score of 150 or more in Tests, before settling down to more mischief. But trying to dismiss a short ball from Panesar through the off side, he got through his stroke too early and dragged onto his stumps. Panesar will not care how the wickets come, but a lower-key celebration, just a skip and jump rather than the normal orgy of self-congratulation, indicated that his 126th Test wicket came as a result of batsman error.

England were immensely pleased to see the Australian captain depart, but, as opening statements go, his innings was a mightily impressive one. Australia's lead stands at 44 and there is plenty of time remaining in the game. England need a good first session on the fourth morning, otherwise it is time to start scanning the forecasts.

Day 4, Saturday 11 July

Close of play: England 435 and 20 for 2; Australia 674 for 6 dec

The rain came all right, great swirling bucketfuls of it in the post-tea session, but not before Australia had extended their lead to 239 and taken two early wickets just before the close. For all the brave talk before the series, it was England's players who were scurrying gratefully to the pavilion when the heavens opened.

It was a day of hundreds, both for Australia and for England, although Australia's came to their batsmen and England's to their bowlers. Marcus North, 54 not out overnight, pushed on to his second Test hundred as did Brad Haddin, the wicket-keeper who is intent on showing that Adam Gilchrist will not be missed.

England's attack suffered the ignominy of completing five hundreds themselves, the first time that has happened since the summer of 1973. At least Andrew Flintoff found some humour in the situation, congratulating each of the bowlers in turn as they passed three figures. In the absence of wickets, a little gallows humour was called for.

England had identified spin as Australia's Achilles' heel before this series began, but it is back to the drawing board, because

Monty Panesar and Graeme Swann looked utterly impotent on a pitch that was spinning, albeit slowly. Between them, England's vaunted duo took one for 246 in 73 overs. Nathan Hauritz has looked the best slow bowler on show.

The day was set up by North and Haddin, who added 200 for the sixth wicket and looked in total control. North has benefited from his experience in England, no doubt, playing for five different counties, but he looks a cricketer in the classic Australian mould: determined, orthodox and tough. Standing tall at the crease, he drives strongly down the ground, flicks nicely off his hips when given the opportunity and, unlike most other Australian batsmen, is happy to sweep the spinners.

He went through to a hundred in three consecutive deliveries off Anderson, and those strokes were a microcosm of his innings as a whole, two flicks through square-leg for two to take him from 94 to 98 and then a glide backward of point for two more, followed by unrestrained joy. He had looked in thoroughly horrible form before the start of this series, until his hundred at Worcester against the Lions, but he is bang in touch now. He could well be an irritation throughout the summer.

Haddin played, if anything, even better, and it was the impetus that he gave to the innings that allowed Ricky Ponting to declare before the weather closed in. Haddin plays in similar fashion to Damien Martyn, the former Australian right-hander, still at the crease, low back-lift and minimum flourish or fuss. He hits the ball as hard as anyone in the Australian team, though, and is always looking to score, so that his hundred came in just 138 balls, 48 of which occupied his second fifty.

Haddin's was the only wicket taken by England all day, and

it came as instructions were sent on to the field to push on. Trying to slap Paul Collingwood over the mid-wicket boundary, he could hit it only as far as Ravi Bopara, waiting and pouching safely. Haddin's job was complete, as was the Australian innings.

Whereas England toiled with the ball, Australia began brightly, Mitchell Johnson hurrying Alastair Cook across his crease and across the line of the ball. Ravi Bopara was a leg-before victim, too, although in this instance there was a touch of misfortune, the ball bouncing from so short of a length that it would surely have gone over the top. Still, Ben Hilfenhaus, looking increasingly like a smart bit of selecting, did not mind.

England began the day 44 adrift and finished it 219 adrift, with just eight wickets in hand. The pitch is worn, but still slow, and it will need at least one innings of magnitude to save this game on the final day.

Day 5, Sunday 12 July

Close of play: England 435 and 252 for 9; Australia 674 for 6 dec

English batsmanship – classic nose-to-the-grindstone, down-in-the-trenches, over-my-dead-body English batsmanship – finally showed its face on the fifth day in Cardiff. And what a welcome sight, in the ruddy features of Paul Collingwood, it was.

Collingwood, unshaven, sunburnt and mired in sweat and dust, batted for 16 minutes shy of six hours, 245 balls of sheer bloody-mindedness and self-restraint, to take England to the brink of safety. Then, as if the cricketing gods had dreamt up the worst torture imaginable, he had to watch from the balcony, fully padded still and full of remorse after not quite seeing the job through, as Monty Panesar and James Anderson blocked out 69 balls to ensure that England go to Lord's on level terms, the Ashes still there for the taking.

A more unlikely pairing with the bat than Anderson and Panesar you could not imagine. They came together with England trailing by six runs still and 11.3 overs remaining. Ricky Ponting turned to Peter Siddle with the second new ball after an erratic spell from Mitchell Johnson, and Siddle had justified his captain's faith by inducing a forcing back-foot drive from Collingwood that ended up in the hands of Mike Hussey in the gully at the second attempt. The champagne corks in the Australia dressing room were ready to pop.

Collingwood's 74 runs were vital, but more important was the attitude and example he showed, both to the dressing room full of batsmen who had made gifts of their wickets earlier in the day and to Anderson and Panesar, who had to make sure that his good work was not wasted. Certainly, Anderson is better than a rabbit these days, but Panesar is a rabbit of *Watership Down* proportions, the kind of tail-ender that pros refer to as a ferret – because they come in after the rabbits.

But somehow they repelled everything that was thrown at them. Siddle, fast and loose-tongued, had a newish ball in his hand; Nathan Hauritz, not exactly the spirit of Shane Warne incarnate but still bowling nicely, was teasing from the Taff End. Anderson lasted for 69 minutes, facing 53 balls in all, and Panesar, remarkably, survived 35 balls.

It didn't feel so at the time, as fingernails were bitten to the quick, but the two survived without any great alarms, only the odd delivery fizzing past the edge as Hauritz's fingers tired after a long day. The biggest danger appeared to be some eccentric running between the wickets.

It was a remarkable end to a Test match that, until the final few hours, had been too one-sided to be considered a classic. But those who were there will not forget the tension as the finishing line approached. Each defensive stroke, each run was cheered to the rafters, the first time, surely, that an English team has had such unqualified support in Wales. With 45 balls remaining, Anderson squeezed Siddle to the off-side boundary twice in consecutive deliveries to take England into the lead and ensure that Australia had to use up two more overs for the change of innings.

Ponting, in desperation, turned to the part-time spin of Marcus North (missing a trick, perhaps, in not trying Michael Clarke's slow left-arm). England, in desperation, began to run down the clock, the twelfth man and the physiotherapist making regular and spurious visits to the middle. The final hour had begun at 5.50 pm; so, at 6.39, with ten minutes needed for the change of innings, Anderson settled down to face the final over of the day from Hauritz, with England leading by just 12. At the end of the over, Australia, after dominating the game, had run out of time, and England, so often in recent times on the receiving end of these agonising draws, had survived. Anderson, Tiger Woods-like, clenched his fist and roared to the gallery.

It had all looked so unlikely in the morning after England had been reduced to 70 for 5 in the first 90 minutes of play. Kevin Pietersen, widely criticised for playing too many shots in England's first innings, decided, as if in a hissy fit, now to play none at all, and was bowled leaving a straight delivery from Ben Hilfenhaus.

Andrew Strauss has an important role to play with Pietersen over the next few days – reassuring, cajoling, bollocking, take your pick – but he needn't have rushed off to the dressing room to chat so soon after Pietersen's dismissal. Attempting to cut Hauritz to the fence for consecutive fours, he edged to Brad Haddin and then had to watch in horror as Matt Prior brainlessly tried to cut a full-length delivery from Hauritz against the grain through point.

Wickets that had come in a rush in the morning came slowly thereafter, like the drip, drip, drip of a tap designed to torture the minds of England supporters. Andrew Flintoff, playing straight until he steered Mitchell Johnson to slip, and Graeme Swann, a coconut shy for Siddle's well-aimed bouncers, played their parts. Either side of tea, Swann discovered a brutal truth as his body and helmet took a battering: that playing against Australia as opposed to West Indies is what first-growth wine is to *vin de table*.

It takes the kind of mental toughness not granted to everyone to withstand cricketers as fiercely proud, committed and skilful as those of Australia. It was a day for substance over style; for bloody-mindedness over brilliance. It was a day for Collingwood.

SCORECARD

ENGLAND v AUSTRALIA
At Sophia Gardens, Cardiff, on 8, 9, 10, 11, 12 July.
Result: **MATCH DRAWN**. Toss: England.

ENGLAND	First Innings	Runs	Mins	Balls	4/6
*A.J.Strauss	c Clarke b Johnson	30	90	60	4
A.N.Cook	c Hussey b Hilfenhaus	10	31	25	–
R.S.Bopara	c Hughes b Johnson	35	76	52	6
K.P.Pietersen	c Katich b Hauritz	69	196	141	4
P.D.Collingwood	c Haddin b Hilfenhaus	64	150	145	6
†M.J.Prior	b Siddle	56	99	62	6
A.Flintoff	b Siddle	37	66	51	6
J.M.Anderson	c Hussey b Hauritz	26	69	40	2
S.C.J.Broad	b Johnson	19	22	20	4
G.P.Swann	not out	47	54	40	6
M.S.Panesar	c Ponting b Hauritz	4	15	17	–
Extras (B 13, LB 11, W 2, NB 12)		38			
Total (106.5 overs; 442 mins)		**435**			

Fall of Wickets: 21-1 (Cook, 7.6 overs); 67-2 (Strauss, 19.6 overs); 90-3 (Bopara, 24.4 overs); 228-4 (Collingwood, 65.3 overs); 241-5 (Pietersen, 70.5 overs); 327-6 (Flintoff, 86.4 overs); 329-7 (Prior, 88.3 overs); 355-8 (Broad, 93.5 overs); 423-9 (Anderson, 102.4 overs); 435-10 (Panesar, 106.5 overs).

AUSTRALIA	Overs	Mdns	Runs	Wkts	Econ	Strike
Johnson	22	2	87	3	3.95	44.0
Hilfenhaus	27	5	77	2	2.85	81.0
Siddle	27	3	121	2	4.48	81.0
Hauritz	23.5	1	95	3	3.98	47.7
Clarke	5	0	20	0	4.00	–
Katich	2	0	11	0	5.50	–

First Test, Cardiff 8–12 July

AUSTRALIA	First Innings	Runs	Mins	Balls	4/6
P.J.Hughes	c Prior b Flintoff	36	61	54	5
S.M.Katich	lbw b Anderson	122	325	261	12
*R.T.Ponting	b Panesar	150	313	224	14/1
M.E.K.Hussey	c Prior b Anderson	3	24	16	–
M.J.Clarke	c Prior b Broad	83	176	145	9/1
M.J.North	not out	125	357	242	13
†B.J.Haddin	c Bopara b Collingwood	121	200	151	11/3
M.G.Johnson					
N.M.Hauritz					
P.M.Siddle					
B.W.Hilfenhaus					
Extras (B 9, LB 14, W 4, NB 7)		34			
Total (6 wkts dec; 181 overs; 724 mins)		**674**			

Fall of Wickets: 60-1 (Hughes, 14.6 overs); 299-2 (Katich, 84.6 overs); 325-3 (Hussey, 90.1 overs); 331-4 (Ponting 94.5 overs); 474-5 (Clarke, 136.5 overs); 674-6 (Haddin, 180.6 overs).

ENGLAND	Overs	Mdns	Runs	Wkts	Econ	Strike
Anderson	32	6	110	2	3.43	96.0
Broad	32	6	129	1	4.03	192.0
Swann	38	8	131	0	3.44	–
Flintoff	35	3	128	1	3.65	210.0
Panesar	35	4	115	1	3.28	210.0
Collingwood	9	0	38	1	4.22	54.0

ENGLAND	Second Innings	Runs	Mins	Balls	4/6
*A.J.Strauss	c Haddin b Hauritz	17	78	54	1
A.N.Cook	lbw b Johnson	6	17	12	1
R.S.Bopara	lbw b Hilfenhaus	1	4	3	–
K.P.Pietersen	b Hilfenhaus	8	20	24	–
P.D.Collingwood	c Hussey b Siddle	74	344	245	6
†M.J.Prior	c Clarke b Hauritz	14	37	32	1
A.Flintoff	c Ponting b Johnson	26	89	71	3
S.C.J.Broad	lbw b Hauritz	14	61	47	1
G.P.Swann	lbw b Hilfenhaus	31	73	63	4
J.M.Anderson	not out	21	69	53	3
M.S.Panesar	not out	7	37	35	1
Extras (B 9, LB 9, W 4, NB 11)		33			
Total (9 wkts; 105 overs; 414 mins)		**252**			

Fall of Wickets: 13-1 (Cook, 4.3 overs); 17-2 (Bopara, 5.3 overs); 31-3 (Pietersen, 10.4 overs); 46-4 (Strauss, 16.6 overs); 70-5 (Prior, 26.3 overs); 127-6 (Flintoff, 49.4 overs); 159-7 (Broad, 66.4 overs); 221-8 (Swann, 86.1 overs); 233-9 (Collingwood, 93.3 overs).

AUSTRALIA	Overs	Mdns	Runs	Wkts	Econ	Strike
Johnson	22	2	44	2	2.00	66.0
Hilfenhaus	15	3	47	3	3.13	30.0
Siddle	18	2	51	1	2.83	108.0
Hauritz	37	12	63	3	1.70	74.0
Clarke	3	0	8	0	2.67	–
North	7	4	14	0	2.00	–
Katich	3	0	7	0	2.33	–

Umpires: Alim Dar (*Pakistan*) (56) and B.R.Doctrove (*West Indies*) (24).
Referee: J.J.Crowe (*New Zealand*) (34). Man of the Match: R.T.Ponting.

Cardiff Test Facts:

- Cardiff was the 100th Test match venue, and the ninth to be used in the UK.

- Ricky Ponting became the 26th man, and the 16th Australian, to score 2000 runs in the Ashes when he reached 22 in his innings.

- This was the first time four or more Australians have scored a century in an innings in an Ashes Test, and the second time in all Tests.

- Simon Katich, Marcus North and Brad Haddin all scored their maiden Ashes centuries.

- Australia's sixth-wicket partnership of 200 was their fifth highest for that wicket in Ashes matches.

- Australia's score of 674 for 6 dec was their highest in an Ashes Test since 1934, and their fourth highest in all Ashes Tests.

Second Test, Lord's
16–20 July

The build-up

Immediately after the Cardiff Test, it emerged that Andrew Flintoff was once again suffering from injury. Whisper it, although not if you happen to find yourself in Preston today, but this is not necessarily bad news for England. That is no longer the kind of heretical statement that would, once upon a time, have brought upon the perpetrator the Inquisition. There is now a general realisation that the talismanic all-rounder of four years ago is no longer as central to England's success as before.

Like a second-hand car with plenty of miles on the clock, Flintoff's body has simply become unreliable. You can give it as many MOTs as you like – and an MOT for Flintoff is another bout of rehabilitation with his physiotherapist and great friend, Dave Roberts – but the fact remains that when you set off on a long journey you are just not quite sure whether you will reach the destination.

His latest setback is a recurrence of the injury to his right knee that he first sustained when plying his trade for Chennai Super Kings in the Indian Premier League. He underwent surgery for a tear in the meniscus at the beginning of the season and missed the opening internationals of the summer and the World Twenty20. This on the back of injuries in the recent past to his hip, which forced him to miss two Test matches in the

Caribbean last winter, and his ankle and side, which shortened his summer last year.

There is no suggestion yet that Flintoff will definitely miss the second Test match. He was sent for a precautionary scan, after complaining of soreness and swelling, but just three days before the second Test, and in the wake of a physically demanding five days at Cardiff, where he bowled 35 overs, he must now be extremely doubtful for Lord's. England will be wary of going into any Test match with a bowler who is not fully fit, nor will they want to risk further injury to Flintoff with three Test matches following in quick succession.

Where does this leave England? Not quite in the hole that some imagine. If Flintoff is not fit then there are two options: the likelier is that the selectors would re-balance the team, bringing in an extra batsman in the shape of the man-boy Ian Bell (who could bat at number six or number three), recalling Steve Harmison and leaving the final decision between Stuart Broad and Graham Onions, there being no place for Monty Panesar on a pitch that was looking green about the gills and damp to the touch.

Less likely is that they would continue to play five bowlers, Harmison as a straight swap for Flintoff, because that would leave England's batting looking too thin with Graeme Swann at seven and Stuart Broad at eight. If, in a four-pronged attack, it comes down to a straight shoot-out between Onions and Broad, there is a good argument for siding with the Durham man, although England will be reluctant to dispense with Broad after one poor match.

Harmison's was the only new name added to the squad for

the second Test announced by the England selectors . Geoff Miller, the national selector, described him as a 'like for like' replacement for Flintoff which is fair enough, up to a point. Both are fast and bouncy, but there is one difference: Harmison has a stack of wickets to his name this season. He has taken 33 in his last five first-class matches alone, at an average of 13.03, including that of Phillip Hughes twice. Flintoff took one for 128 at Cardiff and looked increasingly impotent after a magnificent spell after lunch on the second day. Harmison for Flintoff, then, is a fair swap with the ball.

But what about Flintoff's status as an all-rounder, the runs he scores and the balance that he brings to the side? Flintoff played well in the second innings at Cardiff, responsibly and straight, and he has looked in decent fettle ever since he butchered Derbyshire in a Twenty20 Cup match for Lancashire in June. He is a 'form' player and an in-form Flintoff is an asset to England. But it would be difficult to argue, on the weight of pure runs, that Flintoff is a better batsman than Bell.

Harmison would probably have been picked anyway, with the selectors looking to add some cutting edge to an attack that performed bluntly at Cardiff and, in the unlikely event that Flintoff is fit, there is a chance that both Harmison and Flintoff could play alongside each other, reviving memories, perhaps, of the brutal start to the 2005 Ashes series at Lord's. Australia would, no doubt, remember that they played together through-out the 2006–07 whitewash, too.

So let us move on from the past and from the notion that Flintoff is a talisman for the England team – as the bare statistics suggest we must. Since 2005, England have played 48 Tests, winning 15, losing 16 and drawing 17. Flintoff has missed more than half of those – 25 to be precise – through injury. Without him, England have won 12 matches; in the 23 games that he has played, England have won just three. Flintoff is a fine cricketer, who will and should play if fit, but his stamp is no longer – if it ever has been – a guarantee of success.

England with Flintoff: Strauss, Cook, Bopara, Pietersen, Collingwood, Prior, Flintoff, Swann, Broad, Anderson, Onions

England without Flintoff: Strauss, Cook, Bopara, Pietersen, Collingwood, Bell, Prior, Swann, Anderson, Onions, Harmison.

Even while we were all considering the implications of Andrew Flintoff's injury, and whether or not he would be fit for Lord's, there came news from the England camp that changed our perspectives. The timing of the announcement of Andrew Flintoff's Test match retirement was a bolt out of the azure, coming as it did the day before a vital Ashes Test match, but the news itself came as no surprise. It has been evident for some time that Flintoff's body has been unable to cope with the rigours of bowling in Test cricket, something he himself has now realised.

But as England and Australia went about their business, putting the finishing touches to their preparations, the talk was only of one man. Cameras and notebooks worked furiously in the memorial gardens – jesters in the court of King Flintoff – as the players netted in rare anonymity on the Nursery Ground. It was an odd statement of priorities.

The timing and manner of a player's retirement is for that

player alone, but there is little doubt that Flintoff's news, on the eve of the most important day in the cricketing calendar, was calculated for maximum effect. This is, as he admitted, something he has been thinking about for some time. According to the player, it is an attempt to circumvent any speculation as to his future, but there has been precious little of that. The only speculation has concerned his fitness or otherwise for this Test match.

Alec Stewart and Steve Waugh are notable cricketers in recent years who have announced their retirements early in a summer, both going out in a blaze of glory on their home grounds after weeks of adoration. Other recently retired players, though, have announced theirs with greater consideration: Shane Warne did so at Melbourne in 2006, but only after the Ashes had been won; Glenn McGrath, likewise, a match later. Michael Vaughan announced his this summer before the Ashes began so as not to distract from the bigger picture.

How Flintoff's retirement plays out, depends on how he and England perform. If things go well, at Lord's and beyond, then Flintoff will be the envy of many players who have tried and failed to finish on the highest note. Every run scored, every wicket taken will be greeted in frenzied fashion; every time he walks out on the field, he will carry the affection and thanks of a grateful public. Imagine the roar with which he will be greeted on Thursday morning.

But, as Ricky Ponting pointed out during a round of press conferences during which the match was hardly mentioned, there is the danger that the Flintoff retirement could become a bit of a circus. If things go badly for Flintoff and the team, there will be those who say that selection should be unsentimental and there will be pressure to move on. It is an announcement that has raised the stakes, as if they were not big enough already.

The timing is odd, but it needs to be remembered that Flintoff has just been through another week of pain and injections. Injuries are soul destroying for any sportsman, but especially for one, like Flintoff, who thrives on the sociability and companionship that playing sport offers. Each operation is followed by a period of recuperation, firstly at home, when you are no use to wife or children, and then by lonely hours at the gym and with the physiotherapist who becomes your agony aunt, best mate and worst enemy rolled into one.

Those with the drive and ambition of youth can cope with what is a kind of hell, but for those with money in the bank, fame assured or for those whose glory days are behind them, the process quickly loses its attractions. For all the talk of Flintoff's unprofessionalism – the drinking, the late nights – he has put himself through some incredibly rigorous rehabilitation regimes and has simply lost the will to do it again. 'For two of the last four years I've just spent in rehabilitation and I can't keep doing it for myself, my own sanity and my family,' he said.

Flintoff has always considered himself a batting all-rounder, an assertion seen in some quarters as self-delusional. Certainly, he has had greater impact as a bowler throughout his Test career, but perhaps he suspected all along that his body was more suited to the less rigorous demands of batsmanship and of bowling in one-day cricket.

Ever since his teenage years at Lancashire, when he suffered spinal injuries that prevented him from bowling, his bones have not been able to cope with the jarring that comes from his huge 17 stone frame pounding down on surfaces that have become less cushioned since the covering of pitches and the advent of hard loams. He has never been light on his feet, in the manner of a Michael Holding, nor has he been able to bowl successfully at anything less than full throttle. His spine, hips, knees and ankle have taken a battering and cried enough.

The principal reason for Flintoff's decision, then, is the state of his body, but a contributing factor would be the demands on modern cricketers if they want to play all three forms of the game at the highest level. Earlier in the year, the New Zealand all-rounder Jacob Oram said that it was virtually impossible to be an all-rounder in the modern game, given the intense physical demands. Shane Watson, the Australian all-rounder, is injured; and earlier in the year, Dwayne Bravo, the West Indian all-rounder, was absent from the Test matches.

The advent of domestic Twenty20 leagues providing alternative comforts and increased revenue streams allow for an easy way out. At the beginning of the season, Andrew 'Chubby' Chandler, Flintoff's agent, gave the clearest possible indication that Flintoff and Test cricket were soon to become estranged from each other. It is another wake-up call for the game that must try to balance better its various formats.

Beyond this season, Flintoff will become the first post-modern cricketer. The first, while still playing cricket internationally (he is still available for one-day internationals), to forego all first-class cricket. Instead, he will play one-day cricket for Lancashire, England, the Chennai Super Kings and any other Twenty20 team that can afford him.

The next few weeks, though, will be about enjoying the final moments of Flintoff the Test cricketer. When Bill Woodfull, the great Australian cricketer, retired he did so after a net session at the MCG. 'That's it,' he said after taking off his pads. 'I've had enough.' Flintoff has had enough, but his retirement will be a much more public affair.

In the circumstances, with the series still all-square after England's great escape in Cardiff, there should have been much to discuss. Inevitably, this being Lord's, and England's opponents being Australia, the talk was of the past as well as of an Andrew Flintoff-less future. There was also talk of one-upmanship, as it emerged after Flintoff's press conference that Kevin Pietersen had been given another injection in his Achilles' tendon on Tuesday.

Pietersen also had a further injection in his back before the first Test at Cardiff, which suggests that the injury he picked up in the Caribbean, and aggravated in the Indian Premier League, continues to give him trouble. Either that or he didn't fancy Freddie dominating the news. Ian Bell, the reserve batsman, was released to play for Warwickshire, however, so Pietersen will certainly get his chance in the limelight.

While Bell was allowed to make his way up the M1, there was no release for Stephen Harmison, given the continued uncertainty surrounding Flintoff. Andrew Strauss intimated that the all-rounder was favoured to play, something made more likely, one would have thought, by the timing of the announcement.

England need all the inspirational figures they can muster, given that they have not beaten Australia at Lord's since 1934. Seventy-five years is a long time not to have beaten an opponent you play once in every four on home soil, but, as Strauss said, with the kind of understated irony that Stephen Fry used to good effect at the England captain's benefit dinner the night before, the England team have changed quite a bit in that time.

There have been many reasons put forward for Australia's peculiar dominance at the home of English cricket, most based upon the way the occasion and the venue seem to diminish the home side as much as they inspire the visitors. 'Lord's and its traditions belong just as much to Australia as to England,' John Curtin, the Australian prime minister from 1941 to 1945, once said.

But in recent years, there has been one main reason why Australia have played so well at Lord's, and you don't need to be a history graduate or a student of cultural phenomena to know why. You just need to have watched the Narromine Nagger, otherwise known as Glenn McGrath, create havoc from the Pavilion End. McGrath had an outstanding record at Lord's (26 wickets at 11.50 in three Tests, with three five-wicket hauls) and his absence this year is the biggest reason why England can look forward to greater returns and with greater optimism than before.

It also provides a clue as to whom England should replace Monty Panesar with, given that the pitch looks unlikely to take spin and that the slow left-armer looked unthreatening in Cardiff. McGrath was a line bowler who bowled close to the stumps and who excelled in creating uncertainties in the minds of right-handers who were not sure whether to play – fearing the nip-backer down the slope – or to leave the ball.

The nearest England have to that, and this in no way means that he should be compared to McGrath, is Graham Onions. The Durham fast-medium bowler should, and probably will, come in for Panesar to be given the chance to progress his Test career beyond the two matches he played against the West Indies at the start of the summer. He would bowl well from the Pavilion End and would ask more searching questions of Australia's left-handers than any England bowler bar Flintoff.

Whether he will get the chance to partner Harmison, his county team-mate, is unlikely. If Flintoff plays, Harmison prob-ably will not, although it could be argued that he is more likely to trouble Australia than Stuart Broad on what feels like a firm pitch. But the selectors will not want to drop Broad after one poor match and so Harmison will have to bide his time.

If England have uncertainties over selection then it is because battle plans rarely survive engagement. But, for Ricky Ponting and Australia, things are more settled, the captain hinting that he would name an unchanged side. Ponting is one Australian player not to have been inspired to great deeds at this ground, his top score in Tests being 42. How he would love to poop Freddie's party.

That said, there is no doubt that Ricky Ponting goes into the second Test in a stronger position than his opposite number. Listening to the comments about Ponting before the Ashes began, you would be forgiven for thinking that Australia are being captained by a latter-day J.W.H.T. Douglas, the man who led England to an Ashes whitewash in 1920–21 and whose idea of motivation was to tell one of his players: 'There's no man in England I'd rather bowl to, and none I'd rather bat against.' So what does that make Andrew Strauss, so comprehensively out-manoeuvred by Ponting over five days at Cardiff?

Like complaints of too much noise in a war zone, much of the focus since Cardiff has been on the wrong thing. Yes, there was some gamesmanship (although, in truth, it was remarkable how little time was wasted on the last day); yes, it was done clumsily; but no, Ponting did not go overboard with his post-match criticisms, simply answering a straight question in straightforward fashion – although the next time he harasses an umpire after a decision has gone against his team, you might reflect that there is no need to be lectured by Australia on the 'spirit of the game'.

If Ponting lost the post-match mutterings, there is no doubt who won where it mattered. Other than during the death throes of the match, when the Australian captain's bowling changes could be questioned (why no Michael Clarke and why so little of Ben Hilfenhaus?), there is no doubt that he had the best of the opening rounds. He landed a couple of punches on the England captain who, throughout, appeared more interested in taking the bout to the finish than looking at any stage for the knockout blow.

This may come as news to those who listened to Jeff Thomson's comments about Ponting – 'He's a crap captain and has always been a crap captain'. Thommo's verbal assaults are usually delivered with about as much consideration as his bowling, which, he admitted, was simply the result of shuffling up and going 'whang'. He is also a member of the gang who protect the reputation of Ian Chappell as the finest captain Australia has had and who, like a father who thinks no man is good enough for his daughter, have difficulty in recognising the charms of those who have followed him.

There was, though, another view expressed about Ponting's captaincy by a man who knows a thing or two. A couple of Australian summers ago, when Ponting's captaincy was questioned again after the row between Harbhajan Singh and Andrew Symonds, Richie Benaud was asked to throw his hat into the ring with those suggesting Ponting should be sacked. Benaud not only refused to do so, he offered a strong endorsement of the Australia captain's leadership qualities: 'I think he's done an outstanding job; he's made them hungry to win again.'

Ponting's team certainly looked hungry in Cardiff, testament to the enduring competitive instinct of the captain who said, before the game, that he is as passionate about this series as any he has been involved in. What happens in the dressing room is as important as anything on the field, which makes a captain difficult to evaluate, but it appears from a distance that Ponting has greater empathy with this team than any other he has captained.

Perhaps more than before, he sees this as his team, the young players as his young players, so that he is close to the ideal of 'father confessor as well as an object of fear and inspiration' that the cricket writer Alan Ross described. When South Africa were beaten last winter, Ponting described the victory as his greatest as captain, quite an endorsement when you think that previously he was a part of one of the greatest teams of all time.

He had a particularly good match at Cardiff: got his selections spot on, scored big runs at a decent lick, encouraged his players to up the tempo on the fourth day and then made a brilliant declaration. On recent form, England would have dithered and meandered, as they did twice in the winter in the Caribbean. He played his part in undermining some of England's batsmen, setting excellent fields for Ravi Bopara and Kevin Pietersen, forever buzzing around, adjusting fields and refusing to let batsmen settle.

And Strauss? There were no runs to speak of; there was confusion at the start of Australia's innings when Andrew Flintoff, the team's battering ram, was ignored in favour of Stuart Broad (in whom Strauss had too much faith throughout the game), even though it was clear the plan was to bombard Phillip Hughes, and there was a palpable sense of drift throughout the Australia innings.

This was especially apparent during Saturday's play, as England began the day within touching distance of their opponents and finished with them out of sight. A number of things betrayed the captain's innermost thoughts: the furtive looks to the heavens for the hoped-for rain; the deep-set fields with the second new ball that encouraged a slow death by singles, and the inertia when Monty Panesar was bowling. It might be said that a captain not busy winning is one who is busy losing.

Over the last few months, Strauss's equanimity, his grace under pressure and his phlegmatic nature have been seen to be an important part of the reason why England have recovered so quickly from the Kevin Pietersen/Peter Moores fiasco. Outward serenity is a good thing, providing that it camouflages a mind that is constantly open to the possibilities of the moment rather than one that is blank or fearful of the ultimate outcome.

England's pre-Ashes trip to Ypres was designed to inspire, but as a friend commented to me recently, it was an odd choice, there being no better example in history of lions being led by lambs. Let us hope it was a history lesson Strauss did not take to heart.

Day 1, Thursday 16 July

Close of play: England 364 for 6

For much of the day it was as if England's openers were determined that the remainder of the Ashes series would not just be about Andrew Flintoff. The soon-to-be retired all-rounder sat in the dressing room, surveying the wreckage of a supposedly Test-class Australian attack, and it seemed impossible that he would have to do any work at all. It never pays to rely on England's middle order, though.

As at Cardiff, England did not exactly have a bad opening day, but they did not have a great one, either, wasting a gilt-edged opportunity to hammer a nail in the coffin of Australia's bowling, made threadbare by a serious injury to Nathan Hauritz, who dislocated the middle finger of his bowling hand, and the appalling form of Mitchell Johnson, the strike bowler.

For no apparent reason at all England declined from 221 for 1 to 317 for 5, so that Flintoff found himself walking down the steps of the Long Room and out to a standing ovation with 11 overs remaining. He did not last long, pushing forward to Ben

Hilfenhaus, Australia's best bowler, and edging to second slip, having unfurled only one powerful stroke. He could have one more stab as a Test match batsman at Lord's.

Soon enough there were two more standing ovations. This time, though, they were for present rather than past achievements. Andrew Strauss, a man very much in the prime of his career, went through to 150, and then, shortly after that, walked back to the pavilion, still undefeated with 161 to his name. He played superbly and without him England would not be looking forward to the second day with any optimism.

The Lord's effect, eh? During all the pre-match talk about how Lord's has inspired the Australians to great deeds, it had been forgotten that England's top six have drawn plenty of inspiration of their own from this historic turf. Before yesterday they had scored 12 hundreds at Lord's, three of which had come from the blade of Strauss, who passed 5000 Test runs in his career. The England captain likes to tuck in at Lord's.

He never looked like not adding a fourth yesterday. As badly as Australia bowled to him – and, my, they bowled badly – the England captain gave off an air of utter assurance at the crease, powerfully cutting anything short, clipping clinically off his hips when the bowlers erred in line, his concentration unwavering. His hundred came off the penultimate ball before tea and was celebrated with that usual overhead swing of the bat that belongs on the Centre Court at Wimbledon, and a golden smile.

He offered only two chances. One on 52 to Hauritz, who spilt the firmly hit return drive, then looked down to see his finger at a crooked angle and spent the rest of the afternoon off the field and in pain. Australia are hopeful he will bowl in the second innings. Strauss was also dropped in the gully by Mike Hussey when he had scored 105, a catch that Mr Cricket will, no doubt, flagellate himself all night long for dropping.

These were important runs for Strauss, who had not exactly covered himself with glory at Cardiff. Runs do not guarantee authority, good decision-making or respect – but they sure help. He and Alastair Cook shared in a record opening stand for England against Australia at Lord's, beating the previous best of 182 by the alpha and beta of England openers, Jack Hobbs and Herbert Sutcliffe – a considerable scalp by a pairing some thought too similar in style to succeed.

Cook looked as though he was going to get a hundred of his own, so fluently was he playing and so untroubled did he look. That he did not get there was down to Johnson, who beat the opener for pace and trapped him on the crease five short of three figures. Cook was not unlucky with the decision – he was plumb in front – but he can consider himself unfortunate to get a straight ball from Johnson, who, until then, had fed the openers' favourite cut strokes as if a child desperate for parental admonishment.

For much of the day, Lord's was not so much the best of friends to Australia as the worst of enemies. Only three of them – Ricky Ponting, Michael Clarke and Simon Katich – had played Test cricket on the ground before and after the day, Brad Haddin admitted that many of them had been overawed by the occasion. Nor had their bowlers any experience of the slope. These excuses notwithstanding, Johnson bowled as badly in his first 11 overs, when he conceded 15 boundaries, as any international can have bowled at Lord's in recent times.

When Hauritz left the field, Ponting was effectively down to two main bowlers – Siddle and Hilfenhaus – and Marcus North, the part-timer. Johnson began to find a semblance of form towards the end of the day, but he will become a serious problem for Australia if he continues to bowl as poorly with the new ball. With Ponting's resources stretched thinly, England had the perfect opportunity to banish the profligacy of Cardiff for good.

That they did not was down to a middle order that continues to confuse and confound. Kevin Pietersen played a strange, skittish innings, the kind that suggested all is not well inside the head of England's best batsman. He could have run himself out once, nearly ran out Strauss twice, almost handled the ball as it hovered in the air after a defensive stroke into the ground, and repeatedly flirted at Hilfenhaus's swingers. It came as no surprise when he played across a good one from Siddle.

Ravi Bopara was drawn across his crease by Hilfenhaus; Matt Prior was surprised by some late inswing from Johnson, but would be advised to show less of his stumps to the bowlers, and Paul Collingwood inexplicably crabbed Clarke to mid-on. When Collingwood was out, the England captain had the look of Tiger Woods when Phil Mickelson duffed a drive out of bounds in the Ryder Cup some years ago. It was a look of utter disgust.

Day 2, Friday 17 July

Close of play: England 425; Australia 156 for 8

What had seemed obvious before the start of the series, but was obscured from view at Cardiff, became evident at Lord's again on Friday. For the first time in two decades, England can lay claim to a more potent bowling attack than Australia, a factor that, if the batsmen perform, should bring them a significant advantage in the Ashes.

The disparity between Australia's bowling on the first day, which was blunt and wayward, and England's yesterday, which was for the most part sharp and controlled, should be enough to bring the home team an early lead in the series some time over the next three days, Australia ending another difficult day 156 for 8, still 70 adrift from saving the follow-on.

A 75-year hoodoo is about to be broken unless Ricky Ponting can inspire something miraculous from his team. It has been a terrible two days for him: he spent the first day watching his attack bowl in the manner that would have made a Sydney third-grade side blush, and then the second from the balcony rather than the middle, after a howler from Rudi Koertzen, who gave the Australian captain out caught at slip when replays suggested his bat had clipped his boot and not made contact with the ball.

It was a better day to be an England bowler, for sure. With dark clouds hanging over Lord's, drizzle in the afternoon air, bringing two stoppages totalling 79 minutes, and a pitch that had quickened up overnight, it was a day when ball dominated bat for the first time in the series. The stoppages enabled England's bowlers to stay fresher for longer and forced the batsmen to start over more often than they would have liked.

James Anderson enjoyed the conditions, taking four wickets, the first time he has had an impact (with the ball, at any rate) in an Ashes Test. Andrew Flintoff, rightly given the new ball this time, bowled more quickly than anyone, picking up the key wicket of Mike Hussey, and there was a wicket for Graham Onions and two for Stuart Broad. Australia were rattled by pace, movement and the momentum of the match which turned quickly.

Australia are a resilient bunch and as well as England had bowled and as difficult as the conditions were, Simon Katich and Hussey had taken Australia to 103 for 2, a position of relative safety by mid-afternoon. It took an excellent piece of fielding, rather than bowling, to give England renewed momentum, Broad, running around the Tavern side and diving at full stretch to take a top-edged hook from Katich. It was reminiscent of a catch by Darren Gough in the same corner of the ground, nine years ago, that was the catalyst for a famous victory against West Indies.

Hussey followed eight runs later leaving a straight ball from Flintoff, only to hear the death rattle, and then Michael Clarke chipped Anderson to Alastair Cook, expertly placed at short mid-wicket by Strauss, and Australia were 111 for 5. Marcus North dragged Anderson onto his stumps, chasing his Cardiff hundred with a duck here, Mitchell Johnson pulled Broad to deep square-leg and Brad Haddin miscued to mid-wicket, Cook accepting two more offerings. It was an English-style collapse, 49 for 6 in 15 overs.

Strauss was now lording it on a day that had begun badly for him and his team. Three English wickets fell in the first three overs, including that of the captain, who inexplicably left the second ball of the morning, a straight ball, and failed to add to his overnight score. Four times he has slept on a not-out hundred in Tests and four times he has fallen cheaply the next morning.

Time to bin the early-to-bed ploy and hit the town the next time he overnights on three figures.

It needed a final flourish from Anderson and Onions, and more help-yourself buffet bowling from Johnson, to take England past 400. Ponting had ignored Johnson at the start of the day, and probably wished he had continued to do so when Anderson took him for three fours in an over, and five fours in all. The two put on 47 useful runs before Johnson had Anderson fencing to gully. The wicket enabled Johnson to head to the anonymity of the dressing room, where he could reflect on a Lord's debut that verged on embarrassing. He took three wickets, for sure, but at the extortionate cost of 132 runs in just 21 overs.

Anderson and Flintoff now gave the Australians a lesson in how to bowl with the new ball, a combination of accuracy and menace that must have had Ponting looking on with envy. Australia had 12 overs to survive before lunch, during which time they lost two wickets and looked like losing more.

Hughes unfurled just one crisp, back-foot stroke through point but was shackled by Anderson's length, which was short to him, and his line, which was unerringly straight. It was looking to pull one such delivery that Hughes gloved down the leg-side to Matt Prior, which may be thought of as an unlucky dismissal but which was, in this instance, the result of good bowling and impatient batting.

Anderson had clearly given some thought to how he should bowl to Ponting after Cardiff, because he bowled wider to the Australian captain than before. Accordingly, Ponting was unable to feel bat on ball early on, which he likes to do, and so became fidgety and tense. England's fielders played their part, charging in *en masse* to prevent him from taking a quick single to escape Anderson's threat, and it was shortly afterwards that Anderson got his man.

Koertzen's decision brought a glare from Ponting, but after his strictures at Cardiff he had little choice but to turn smartly on his heels. Soon afterwards, he was seen introducing his team, gamely with a smile, to the Queen. One trusts she did not ask of his day.

Day 3, Saturday 18 July

Close of play: England 425 and 311 for 6; Australia 215

If Andrew Strauss glances at the Sunday newspapers, he might wonder which team is 521 runs to the good. It is England, of course, led by their increasingly assured captain. Not that you would know it, to judge from some of the reactions to his decision not to enforce the follow-on, when Australia were bowled out still ten runs shy of forcing England to bat again.

England will win the game regardless of the decision to bat again, taken understandably by Strauss after Australia had added 59 runs for their last two wickets in the first 14 overs of the morning. They would probably win either way, such is England's dominance right now, but things looked pretty flat in the morning, and the rest will no doubt do Andrew Flintoff's knee some good, even though he was spared bowling duties at the start of the day.

Nobody has scored more than 418 in the final innings of a

Test match to win the game and the best run chase at Lord's is a paltry 344. So if Strauss does not extend England's innings this morning, he has Australia exactly where he wants them – at his and Flintoff's mercy, even if the pitch is still playing well.

It would be difficult to describe England's progress yesterday as dominant, but it was a workmanlike performance, in a professional getting-the-job-done kind of way. All the batsmen got in, and, frustratingly, a few got out before they were able to put Australia on to the defensive completely. But with half-centuries for Paul Collingwood and the fluent Matt Prior, and contributions from the top four, the gains of the first two days have not been wasted.

Kevin Pietersen played a curious innings, 44 in (for him) double-slow time, a reflection perhaps on his physical state, which gets more precarious by the day. He has spent increasing amounts of time off the field throughout this game, struggled to find his long stride forward at the crease and hobbled his runs. He is far from fully fit and may struggle to see the series through.

Pietersen was one of two wickets for Peter Siddle, the other four coming courtesy of a direct hit run-out from Marcus North to end Prior's stay, and three for Nathan Hauritz. It was Hauritz who struck first as Alastair Cook played across the line, not for the first time, and then he produced a beauty to Strauss that floated and then spun across Strauss's attempted drive. There was nothing so mesmeric about his delivery to get rid of Ravi Bopara, a nothing delivery that Bopara helped to Simon Katich at short-leg. Bopara will be furious with himself for getting a start and then getting out in such a soft manner.

With Hauritz and Siddle in the wickets, there was another blank day for Mitchell Johnson, who is fast becoming, along with

Phillip Hughes, a worry for Australia. Johnson's inaccuracy and poor form look increasingly costly with every day that passes after Cardiff, where he really ought to have been able to knock over one of Monty Panesar or James Anderson, and perhaps that failure of nerve is playing on his mind. He did put in an improved spell just before tea when he might have added Bopara's scalp to his list.

It wasn't an easy day for Ricky Ponting either, who is fast becoming the Australian the crowds love to hate. They weren't happy yesterday when he appeared to query Rudi Koertzen after a catch claimed by Hauritz was referred to the third umpire. Ponting has history in this regard, although he will feel aggrieved given Koertzen's decision when he was batting the day before.

Still, the crowd was not for taking context into account when they gave Australia's captain the bird, their delight increased further when he missed a run-out opportunity, mis-fielded and dropped a sitter at slip off Bopara. Ponting is a tough little nut, but this tour is shaping up as a serious test of character. No Australian captain has been on the losing side here for three-quarters of a century, and the knowledge that defeat is coming will be difficult for Ponting to deal with.

Day 4, Sunday 19 July

Close of play: England 425 and 311 for 6 dec; Australia 215 and 313 for 5

For much of yesterday, Australia resembled a man hanging from a cliff by his fingernails, clawing and scraping the rock face, but slipping ever more gradually into the abyss. That they had defied gravity by the end of the day was down solely to the brilliance and fighting spirit of Michael Clarke and Brad Haddin, who put on a record sixth-wicket partnership for Australia at Lord's, and who have given their team a glimmer of hope when all had seemed lost.

Australia had been outplayed, out-thought and out-fought until Clarke, who scored his third Ashes hundred and his first in England, and Haddin came together at 128 for 5, the game seemingly beyond them and England rampant. But Test-match victories against Australia do not come cheap and, if anything, it was England who were grateful for the chance to recuperate when the umpires offered the light with 12 overs remaining in the day, the partnership worth an unbeaten 185.

Strauss had already called his team together for an unscripted team talk when the new ball was taken after 80 overs. Was this the first signs of panic, with Australia still 245 adrift, or was it the officer rallying his troops for one more push into enemy territory? Whatever it was, it did not work as Clarke and Haddin continued to attack, 26 runs coming in the final six overs of the day. Strauss will have been grateful for the night's rest, which should invigorate his seam attack and force the batsmen to start again.

Australia still require 209 to win. Memories of Edgbaston 2005, when Australia came close to winning from an impossible situation, remain sharp, the pitch is good and Australia bat deep. England's alpha males, Andrew Flintoff and Kevin Pietersen, are hurting, to judge from the amount of time they are spending off the field, and Graham Onions is also not fully fit, having hurt his elbow. But an early wicket should seal Australia's fate; England should win, and win comfortably.

They will have to separate the two New South Welshmen, though, Clarke and Haddin, who played magnificently. Clarke represents the aristocracy of Australian batting, light of frame, all twinkling footwork, supple wrists and positive intent. His off-side driving at the start of his innings yesterday was a delight, his down-the-pitch style of play against the off spin of Graeme Swann a lesson. Haddin is stockier in build, his strokes punchy rather than silky smooth; he is worth his place in the side as a batsman alone and he won't be bullied.

Both had to be resilient after England's bowlers had once again showed Australia how best to exploit what has been an excellent Test pitch. One of the reasons behind England's improved showing has been the decision to give Andrew Flintoff the new ball and he led the way again with an initial spell of 7-2-9-2 that pinned Australia to the back foot – literally and metaphorically – from the word go.

Even when he was not taking wickets, he was softening up the batsmen at the other end. Swann's castling of Marcus North with a lovely drifter owed much to the treatment handed out by Flintoff during his seven-over afternoon spell. Stuart Broad took his cue from Flintoff's leadership and bowled his best spell of the series after lunch, sustained pressure at last from him that culminated in the wicket of Ricky Ponting, dragging onto his stumps from wide.

Ponting's dismissal was the only one of the first four wickets to fall that involved no controversy. Rudi Koertzen failed to spot that Flintoff had overstepped the mark before Simon Katich drove fatally to gully and then refused to refer to the third umpire Phillip Hughes's edge after Andrew Strauss dived forward to scoop or catch the ball, depending on your point of view. Mike Hussey was then adjudged by Billy Doctrove to have been caught at first slip off Swann when replays suggested he hit the ground but not the ball.

Hughes's was the most controversial of the three dismissals, the Australian captain urging his 20-year-old opener to stand his ground while the umpires conferred. Had Koertzen referred the catch, the third umpire, Nigel Llong, would, surely, not have been able to conclude for certain that the ball had carried to Strauss. The catch was probably good, but replays served only to muddy the waters.

Koertzen has not had a particularly good match, erroneously giving the Australian captain out in the first innings, and showing a lack of consistency now, given that he had referred a 'catch' by Nathan Hauritz in England's second innings. But two things need to be said in his defence: he is not the first umpire to miss a no-ball and a millimetre makes no difference to whether the batsman edges the ball or not. And, if every such catch were referred, no batsman would be given out, since, because of the foreshortening of the image, the cameras often lie.

The controversy shrouded one or two other things, too: Hughes's eccentric technique at the top of the order is unravelling by the hour, highlighting what a risk it was by the Australia selectors to come with only two specialist openers, and what a difference it would have made to Flintoff's tally of Test wickets if, as on these two occasions, he had bowled a consistently fuller length. He found the edge of both Hughes and

Katich by drawing them forward, something he has conspicuously failed to do for most of his career.

No doubt there will be much whingeing Down Under after this, as there was in 2005 about the rub of the green. England felt the rub went against them in 2006–07 and for most of the 1990s. It pays to remember that better bowling attacks create more chances, and therefore create more opportunities for the umpires to make mistakes. England feel that they hold more arrows in their quiver than Australia, which the bowlers must prove this morning as a pre-sold full house gathers to see Australia's Lord's spell broken.

Day 5, Monday 20 July

Close of play: England 425 and 311 for 6 dec;
Australia 215 and 406

Miracles rarely happen in sport – just ask Tom Watson. Making more runs to win than any other team has ever made in the fourth innings of a first-class game proved beyond Australia yesterday. They bowed down not to history, though, but to Andrew Flintoff.

Flintoff was the plot, the subplot, the chapter headings and the footnotes of the 21 overs it took England to bury 75 years of Ashes hurt at Lord's. Bowling unchanged for ten overs from the Pavilion End, as quickly and with as much hostility as any England bowler has mustered in recent times, he took three of the last five wickets to fall, giving him his first five-wicket haul at Lord's.

The sight of Australia batsmen clearly brings out the best in him, as do the grandest of occasions. It was at The Oval in 2005, the match when the Ashes were decided, that Flintoff last took five wickets in an innings of any match and there has been no grander stage for him since than yesterday morning, with Lord's bursting at the seams and Australia at England's mercy.

For some reason, even though the touring team began the day five wickets down and 209 runs adrift, it was commonly felt to be squeaky bum time. They couldn't lose this, could they? To ease frayed overnight nerves, England needed a strong start and Flintoff and James Anderson, who bowled a superb opening over to Michael Clarke, gave them just that, as they had done throughout the game.

It took Flintoff only four balls to strike, moving one fractionally up the hill to find the edge of Brad Haddin's bat, the wicket-keeper unable to add to his overnight score. A wicket maiden. Nine more Flintoff overs followed, each as hostile and as threatening as the last. Clarke took a blow to the back of the head; Mitchell Johnson numerous to the arms, shoulder and body. A thunderbolt burst through Matt Prior's gloves.

When Nathan Hauritz shouldered arms and heard the clatter of leather on stump, Flintoff stood in the middle of the pitch, legs splayed, arms raised aloft. He was mobbed. When, 25 runs later, he castled Peter Siddle with a similar delivery, to ensure his name would be on the honours board for posterity, he knelt down on one knee in the middle of the pitch, head bowed, as if about to be knighted. He was mobbed again. He rose up through the clamour of his team-mates and saluted each corner of the ground in turn, with a special nod to the Grand Stand where the WAGs were sitting.

The only surprise was that the winning moment did not fall to him. That pleasure belonged to Graeme Swann instead, brought into the attack at the Nursery End after three overs apiece from Anderson and Stuart Broad. Swann had effectively sealed Australia's fate when, with his second delivery, he somehow persuaded Clarke to skip down and miss a full toss, the right-hander leaving the stage – still dazzled from his batting the night before – for 136, and it was Swann who brought the curtain down when Johnson swiped across the line and was bowled: four wickets for the lead singer of Dr Comfort and the Lurid Revelations.

The margin of victory, then, was 115 runs, the gulf between the teams even wider than this suggests. Ricky Ponting, gracious and honest in defeat as he was in near-victory at Cardiff, acknowledged his team's shortcomings and will be grateful for the nine-day hiatus that will give his team the opportunity to regroup. He knows that holding the Ashes confers an in-built advantage (a little like an away goal in football), but that his bowlers will have to improve substantially if his team are to retain the Ashes.

Critics may look to Australia's first innings, when they lost six wickets for 49 runs to concede a huge first-innings lead, in explaining their defeat. In reality, though, the bowling is by far the bigger problem. Australia, after all, are yet to win a first-class game on tour: they couldn't bowl out Sussex in 89 overs second time around, nor could they knock England over at Cardiff, despite having them five down at lunch on the final day, and they rarely looked dangerous at Lord's.

Johnson remains the biggest problem, leaking runs with the

new ball without threatening, and will have to play for his place at Northampton where the tourists go next. They will hope that Brett Lee and Shane Watson are fit enough to provide them with options if Johnson cannot relocate his radar, as Stuart Clark is said to have lost his nip. Phillip Hughes could do with a few runs to remind himself that batting can be fun.

England will also be happy for the break, Andy Flower, the team director, admitting post-match concerns about the fitness of Flintoff and Kevin Pietersen. Flower said that Pietersen was in constant discomfort and that he would be unhappy going into a Test match with Flintoff if he could not guarantee his fitness over five days. Stephen Harmison, who took six wickets in the shires during this Test, and Monty Panesar will be discussed, as will Graham Onions' contribution in this match and the Edgbaston pitch.

That is for the future, though. This will be remembered as Flintoff's match. He began it by announcing his retirement from Test cricket; he finished it by revealing, if we didn't already know, how much he will be missed.

SCORECARD

ENGLAND v AUSTRALIA

At Lord's, London, on 16, 17, 18, 19, 20 July.
Result: **ENGLAND won by 115 runs.** Toss: England.

ENGLAND	First Innings	Runs	Mins	Balls	4/6
*A.J.Strauss	b Hilfenhaus	161	370	268	22
A.N.Cook	lbw b Johnson	95	190	147	18
R.S.Bopara	lbw b Hilfenhaus	18	20	19	4
K.P.Pietersen	c Haddin b Siddle	32	38	42	4
P.D.Collingwood	c Siddle b Clarke	16	43	36	1
†M.J.Prior	b Johnson	8	13	10	2
A.Flintoff	c Ponting b Hilfenhaus	4	16	10	1
S.C.J.Broad	b Hilfenhaus	16	50	26	2
G.P.Swann	c Ponting b Siddle	4	6	6	1
J.M.Anderson	c Hussey b Johnson	29	47	25	5
G.Onions	not out	17	40	29	2
Extras (B 15, LB 2, NB 8)		25			
Total (101.4 overs; 425 mins)		**425**			

Fall of Wickets: 196-1 (Cook, 47.5 overs); 222-2 (Bopara, 53.6 overs); 267-3 (Pietersen; 65.1 overs); 302-4 (Collingwood, 76.3 overs); 317-5 (Prior, 79.3 overs); 333-6 (Flintoff, 82.3 overs); 364-7 (Strauss, 90.2 overs); 370-8 (Swann, 91.5 overs); 378-9 (Broad, 92.6 overs); 425-10 (Anderson, 101.4 overs).

AUSTRALIA	Overs	Mdns	Runs	Wkts	Econ	Strike
Hilfenhaus	31	12	103	4	3.32	46.5
Johnson	21.4	2	132	3	6.09	43.3
Siddle	20	1	76	2	3.80	60.0
Hauritz	8.3	1	26	0	3.05	–
North	16.3	2	59	0	3.57	–
Clarke	4	1	12	1	3.00	24.0

Second Test, Lord's 16–20 July

AUSTRALIA	First Innings	Runs	Mins	Balls	4/6
P.J.Hughes	c Prior b Anderson	4	10	9	1
S.M.Katich	c Broad b Onions	48	141	93	6
*R.T.Ponting	c Strauss b Anderson	2	19	15	–
M.E.K.Hussey	b Flintoff	51	127	91	8
M.J.Clarke	c Cook b Anderson	1	21	112	–
M.J.North	b Anderson	0	33	14	–
†B.J.Haddin	c Cook b Broad	28	28	38	3
M.G.Johnson	c Cook b Broad	4	13	11	1
N.M.Hauritz	c Collingwood b Onions	24	53	36	4
P.M.Siddle	c Strauss b Onions	35	65	47	5
B.W.Hilfenhaus	not out	6	20	14	1
Extras (B 4, LB 6, NB 2)		12			
Total (63 overs; 267 mins)		**215**			

Fall of Wickets: 4-1 (Hughes, 2.3 overs); 10-2 (Ponting, 6.6 overs); 103-3 (Katich, 32.4 overs); 111-4 (Hussey, 35.6 overs); 111-5 (Clarke, 36.3 overs); 139-6 (North, 42.3 overs); 148-7 (Johnson, 45.5 overs); 152-8 (Haddin, 47.5 overs); 196-9 (Hauritz, 58.3 overs); 215-10 (Siddle, 62.6 overs).

ENGLAND	Overs	Mdns	Runs	Wkts	Econ	Strike
Anderson	21	5	55	4	2.61	31.5
Flintoff	12	4	27	1	2.25	72.0
Broad	18	1	78	2	4.33	54.0
Onions	11	1	41	3	3.72	22.0
Swann	1	0	4	0	4.00	–

ENGLAND	Second Innings	Runs	Mins	Balls	4/6
*A.J.Strauss	c Clarke b Hauritz	32	64	48	4
A.N.Cook	lbw b Hauritz	32	54	42	6
R.S.Bopara	c Katich b Hauritz	27	136	93	4
K.P.Pietersen	c Haddin b Siddle	44	156	101	5
P.D.Collingwood	c Haddin b Siddle	54	121	80	4
†M.J.Prior	run out	61	50	42	9
A.Flintoff	not out	30	34	27	4
S.C.J.Broad	not out	0	1	0	–
G.P.Swann					
J.M.Anderson					
G.Onions					
Extras (B 16, LB 9, W 1, NB 5)		31			
Total (6 wkts dec; 71.2 overs; 317 mins)		**311**			

Fall of Wickets: 61-1 (Cook, 14.1 overs); 74-2 (Strauss, 16.2 overs); 147-3 (Bopara, 44.4 overs); 174-4 (Pietersen, 51.1 overs); 260-5 (Prior, 63.2 overs); 311-6 (Collingwood, 71.2 overs).

AUSTRALIA	Overs	Mdns	Runs	Wkts	Econ	Strike
Hilfenhaus	19	5	59	0	3.10	–
Johnson	17	2	68	0	4.00	–
Siddle	15.2	4	64	2	4.17	46.0
Hauritz	16	1	80	3	5.00	32.0
Clarke	4	0	15	0	3.75	–

AUSTRALIA	Second Innings	Runs	Mins	Balls	4/6
P.J.Hughes	c Strauss b Flintoff	17	46	34	2
S.M.Katich	c Pietersen b Flintoff	6	15	5	1
*R.T.Ponting	b Broad	38	88	69	6
M.E.K.Hussey	c Collingwood b Swann	27	100	63	3
M.J.Clarke	b Swann	136	313	227	14
M.J.North	b Swann	6	26	25	1
†B.J.Haddin	c Collingwood b Flintoff	80	187	130	10
M.G.Johnson	b Swann	63	94	75	9
N.M.Hauritz	b Flintoff	1	5	5	–
P.M.Siddle	b Flintoff	7	18	13	1
B.W.Hilfenhaus	not out	4	11	4	–
Extras (B 5, LB 8, NB 8)		21			
Total (107 overs; 459 mins)		**406**			

Fall of Wickets: 17-1 (Katich, 3.1 overs); 34-2 (Hughes, 9.2 overs); 78-3 (Ponting, 23.4 overs); 120-4 (Hussey, 32.4 overs); 128-5 (North, 38.4 overs); 313-6 (Haddin, 87.4 overs); 356-7 (Clarke, 98.2 overs); 363-8 (Hauritz, 99.4 overs); 388-9 (Siddle, 103.6 overs); 406-10 (Johnson, 106.6 overs).

ENGLAND	Overs	Mdns	Runs	Wkts	Econ	Strike
Anderson	21	4	86	0	4.09	–
Flintoff	27	4	92	5	3.40	32.4
Onions	9	0	50	0	5.56	–
Broad	16	3	49	1	3.06	96.0
Swann	28	3	87	4	3.11	42.0
Collingwood	6	1	29	0	4.83	–

Umpires: B.R.Doctrove (*West Indies*) (25) and R.E.Koertzen (*South Africa*) (99). Referee: J.J.Crowe (*New Zealand*) (35). Man of the Match: A.Flintoff.

Lord's Test Facts:

- This was England's first Ashes victory at Lord's since 1934, their only win there in the twentieth century.

- England's first-wicket partnership of 196 in the first innings was their highest in Ashes Tests at Lord's.

- Andrew Strauss's 161 in the first innings was his third Ashes century and his fourth at Lord's, where only Graham Gooch and Michael Vaughan have scored more.

- England's tenth-wicket partnership of 47 in the first innings was their highest in Ashes Tests at Lord's.

- Australia's sixth-wicket partnership of 185 in the second innings was their highest at Lord's.

- Michael Clarke's 136 in the second innings was his third Ashes hundred, and the highest score by an Australian at Lord's since 1993.

- Andrew Flintoff's five for 92 was only his fourth five-wicket haul in first-class cricket, but his second against Australia.

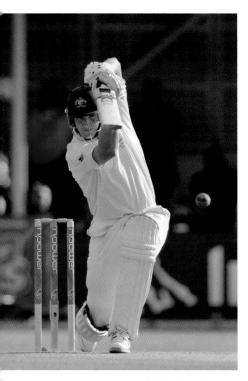

Shane Watson immediately proved his worth as a makeshift opener on the truncated first day at Edgbaston, making 62 not out in the 30 overs that were possible.

ut he was dismissed immediately on the second morning by Graham Onions, who got ngland off to the best possible start by taking two wickets with his first two balls.

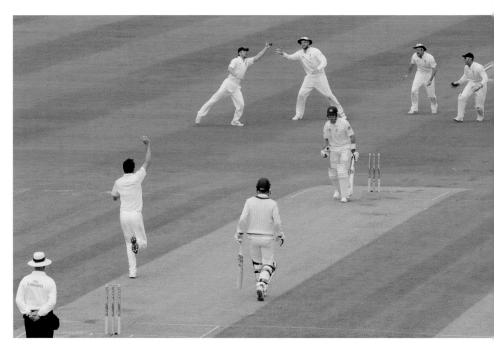

On his debut, Graham Manou got an almost unplayable ball from James Anderson to leave Australia struggling at 203 for 8.

The Saturday at Edgbaston was a complete washout, with the outfield resembling a lake despite all the efforts of the groundstaff.

Matt Prior played another crucial innings in the middle of the order for England. With Andrew Flintoff, he turned the balance of the Test in England's favour.

When Graeme Swann bowled Ricky Ponting with a beauty that turned sharply late on the fourth day to leave Australia at 52 for 2, it seemed that everything was set up for a dramatic final day.

Michael Clarke on his way to another century as he batted for most of the day to ensure Australia drew the Test.

Andrew Flintoff recovers after stumbling in his delivery stride on the last day at Edgbaston. Increasing concerns about his fitness meant that he would miss the fourth Test.

The flags are waving, 'Jerusalem' is being sung, but after all the pre-match confusion, England are about to find that the balance of the series will swing again.

Having been lucky to survive a good shout for LBW first ball, Andrew Strauss isn't so lucky this time as Marcus North takes a great catch in the slips off Peter Siddle.

Stuart Clark may have lost a little of his nip, but he gave a brilliant demonstration on the first day of how to bowl at Headingley. Here he has Alastair Cook caught at slip by Michael Clarke.

Ricky Ponting pulls Stephen Harmison for four as he helped his side into the lead after England had been bowled out for a feeble 102.

Marcus North celebrates after hitting Graeme Swann for six to bring up his second century of the series.

Mike Hussey's disappointing series continues as he falls LBW to Stuart Broad, who returned his best-ever Test figures of 6 for 91, a rare highlight for England.

Ravi Bopara might have been unlucky with his second-innings dismissal, but a record of 105 runs in seven innings batting at number three led to him being dropped for the final Test.

Ian Bell falls to the bowling of Mitchell Johnson for the second time in the Test, well held by Ricky Ponting; Johnson looked ominously back in form.

Stuart Broad lofts Stuart Clark back over his head as the England lower order tried to restore some dignity to England's performance.

Third Test, Birmingham

30 July–3 August

The build-up

England can still win the Ashes without Kevin Pietersen. The news that a couple of days after the Lord's Test he has had surgery on his troublesome Achilles' tendon injury and will miss the next six weeks is a devastating blow for him personally and a big one for the team. Against the most moderate Australian bowling outfit for two decades, though, it should not be an insurmountable one.

Andy Flower clearly knew the news was coming when, in bullish mood after the win at Lord's, the England team director intimated that neither Pietersen nor Andrew Flintoff was essential to the team's ultimate victory. He was softening the blow and while he was right to stress that they are not essential, he knows also that the absence of one or both makes the job much harder.

Pietersen has obviously been struggling for some time, cortisone injections masking the pain but not the problem. Questions will be raised again as to his participation in the Indian Premier League, a tournament that took place after the batsman had suffered initial problems with his Achilles' tendon in the Caribbean last winter. That now seems like it was the ideal time to have rested.

His form has certainly been affected by his lack of mobility. Pietersen's running at Lord's, always eccentric, verged on the schizophrenic, his body unable to do his mind's bidding. He turned an easy three into a two just before his second-innings dismissal and paid the penalty. And while he was committed and proud enough to make the top score in the first innings at Cardiff and 44 in the second innings at Lord's, the runs were not scored in the manner we have come to expect. Watching Pietersen is usually a pleasure; at Lord's it was almost purgatory.

This would have been partly down to the physical effects of his injury, the inability perhaps fully to push forward as he likes to do, but also the mental challenge needed to overcome the knowledge that something out of your control is inhibiting top-class performance. Playing with a serious injury is just about the hardest thing in sport.

He will be missed for three reasons: his performances against Australia have always been excellent, as his record of 1116 runs in just a dozen Test matches suggests; he is the one man in the England team that Ricky Ponting knows can take the game away from his bowlers, and he is the ultimate big-match player. As this series nears its conclusion, and as nerves become frayed and expectations increase, big-match players are essential.

England are fortunate to have a high-calibre replacement in Ian Bell, although should there be any more injuries, or indeed a prolonged loss of form from Ravi Bopara, it is not clear who would be the next in line. Mark Ramprakash's time has surely gone; Michael Vaughan has gone and Robert Key has had a poor season, although he could well be running into form at the right time. Owais Shah would be the next best option, and after that a young gun such as Joe Denly.

If ever a bell tolled for a batsman, though, now is the time. Ian, of that name, paid the price for a horribly casual shot in the second innings of the Jamaica debacle in February and has had nothing more than a watching brief since. He has been kept in the frame, though, travelling around as the spare batsman and captaining the Lions, without any conspicuous personal success, against the touring team at Worcester. The selectors should benefit from that consideration and foresight.

Bell has not had a great deal of success against Australia, averaging 25 against them. Somehow he has never quite risen to the challenge and, this is difficult to quantify, he has never quite looked like doing so. He is, however, in good form, having scored a century in the LV County Championship against Lancashire at the same time as the Lord's Test, and he will benefit from the home comforts of Edgbaston. He is a top-class player and should view this second coming as an opportunity to prove the doubters, and Australia, wrong. Against this attack, he will never have a better chance.

It is unlikely that he will bat at first drop, since Bopara has prior claim there. Slipping in at number four would cause least disruption, although his best performances have come lower down the order. There is no doubt that the line-up has a more fragile feel now, with Bopara being tested in his first Ashes series, Bell returning, and Matt Prior at number six.

This news will certainly give Ponting and his team a lift after a difficult few days. A more pressing concern is the form of his bowlers. If they continue to perform as they did at Lord's then Pietersen's absence should not matter.

But if England think they have problems, with the loss of Kevin Pietersen and concerns about the fitness of Andrew Flintoff, they go into the third Test match in the happier position. As Flintoff knows all too well, careers are made during Ashes series. They can be destroyed, too. Mitchell Johnson and Phillip Hughes came with reputations that were inversely proportionate to the length and breadth of their achievements and the most worrying sound for Australia during the first two Tests has been the gentle hiss of escaping air as their balloon-like reputations deflate.

Forget the fitness of Brett Lee and Shane Watson or the state of mind of Ricky Ponting, Johnson and Hughes are Australia's biggest problems right now and they will not retain the Ashes unless a cure is established. More than that, if they continue to perform poorly or if alternatives are not found, not only will Australia lose the Ashes, they will also lose the series heavily.

At the moment, it does not matter whether Ponting wins or loses the toss, it does not matter which team bat or bowl first; England know that, from the outset, they have an advantage. It is why great opening batsmen and opening bowlers really are worth double, because they settle dressing-room nerves at the outset and set the tone for the rest of the match.

The numbers tell Hughes's tale, as they do for any batsman. Since the opening match, against Sussex at Hove, his top score has been 36. But much more damaging for Australia is his very obvious discomfort against the short ball. From the moment Stephen Harmison did his patriotic duty for England Lions at Worcester and sent down two bouncers on the perfect line, the word has gone around that Hughes has a problem. He is small in stature, something that has not proved to be a disadvantage to generations of batsmen, but when things are going badly he lacks the physical presence of, say, a Matthew Hayden. He looks intimidated, not intimidating.

Specifically, he also has a technical problem. His back foot splays to the leg side on delivery, an involuntary twitch that is fiendishly difficult to shake off, so that the angle of his hips, shoulders and his body face mid-off and not the bowler. It means that he has a blind spot on anything on ribcage or armpit line. Nor does he find it easy to score on the leg side, since his hips are 'closed' and in the way, and his bat cannot get at the ball.

Out of desperation in the first innings at Lord's, he tried to counter by using the pull stroke, clearly not one of his strengths, and gloved a catch down the leg side. Now he does not know whether to stick or twist; if he ducks, his scoring options are limited and the score stagnates, but if he pulls, he takes an unnecessary risk.

Of course, it needs accuracy from the bowlers to pin him down, and that is why Andrew Strauss was right to give Flintoff the new ball instead of Stuart Broad. With Flintoff providing James Anderson with the best possible support, England dominated the opening salvos, especially because Simon Katich, good player that he is, is an accumulator rather than an aggressor. Hughes was supposed to take the pressure off Katich rather than increase it and the selectors have nowhere to go after they decided to bring only two specialist openers on tour.

Despite taking eight wickets in two Tests, Johnson is even more of a problem than Hughes, because a batsman who has a bad day can escape to the safety and privacy of the pavilion, whereas a bowler's torment is a very public one and can last all day, or all five days in Johnson's case. He is guilty of not only lacking cutting edge with the new ball, but also spraying it around, so that England get off to the kind of flyer that Hughes was supposed to give Australia.

Like Hughes, Johnson has technical issues. His head is falling away too soon, his arm is too low, so that his wrist is not behind the ball, precluding any chance of swing. With such a low arm, the margin for error on the timing of the release is non-existent, low arms producing wild variations of length and line. Troy Cooley, Australia's celebrated bowling coach, has a short amount of time to work some magic.

Cooley can help with technique, but may not be able to help with Johnson's state of mind, which veered from frustrated to obviously embarrassed as the Lord's Test progressed. Hands on hips, peering at the heavens and just occasionally issuing a barbed comment to the batsman, as if to remind himself that he is a fast bowler, Johnson increasingly reminded observers of Chris Matthews, the scattergun left-armer who played briefly for Australia in the 1986–87 series.

There was another reminder at Lord's of the dog days of the mid-1980s for Australia. Allan Border, weather-beaten, diminutive and proud, had a watching brief during the second Test and it is only those of Border's vintage who can remember a time that Australia had such a modest bowling attack. In 1985, Border was helpless as England's batsmen gorged themselves on hapless bowling, powerless, like Ponting at Lord's, to do anything about it.

The Australia selectors at least have some options with their bowling. Brett Lee, when fit, will challenge, although it should be remembered that his record against England and in England is modest for a bowler with more than 300 Test wickets. If picked at number six ahead of Marcus North, Shane Watson could add more ballast, while Stuart Clark will surely get a run-out against Northamptonshire. Perhaps Clark and Ben Hilfenhaus with the new ball, and Johnson and Lee with the old, would be Australia's strongest line-up, although that would mean batting Brad Haddin at number six, which they will be loath to do.

There is a tendency in England, born out of years of bitter experience, to imagine that every young cricketer who appears from country towns like Macksville (Hughes) and Townsville (Johnson) must be a cricketing genius. Reputation or reality? Three matches to find out.

If the 2009 Ashes series has so far lived up to the expectations created by the drama in 2005, England will be very aware that the roles have been neatly reversed. It is Australia, not England, who go to Edgbaston 1-0 down, but it is England who have just suffered their 'Glenn McGrath moment' with the Achilles' tendon injury to Kevin Pietersen.

When McGrath stepped on a ball before the start of the first day at Edgbaston in 2005, it was widely considered to be the moment that the tide turned. What McGrath's injury obscured, though, was how complacent Australia had become before then – something England should not be guilty of repeating.

After Australia won the first Test at Lord's in 2005, Ricky Ponting was heard to say that a whitewash could be on the cards, that the series would be no different to any of the previous seven, and subsequently the Australians barely lifted a finger between

Lord's and Edgbaston. While Andy Flower will have been glad to give his charges a break after two nerve-jangling Test matches, the England team director knows that the hard work has to begin again and there can be no room for complacency.

If the injury to Pietersen can be tailored to suit the needs of the England team, it is that it will enable Flower to demand a redoubling of efforts. An injury to a star player can be debilitating, as it was for Australia in 2005, but it can also produce a greater determination and unity from those who remain. Into this situation, and the need for greater responsibility to be taken, steps Ian Bell, recalled to the team in place of Pietersen.

Bell's return will be greeted with an indifferent shrug because it was long expected. After his demotion in the wake of the second-innings debacle at Sabina Park in February, he was continually name-checked by Miller, the national selector, whenever the opportunity arose, so it was clear that he had not been banished to the wastelands of county cricket for good. He also benefited from continued association with the senior team and from promotion to captaining England Lions. He has overtaken Owais Shah, who replaced Bell in the Caribbean, almost by stealth.

The indifference stems partly from this lack of surprise, but also because English cricket supporters are yet to take Bell completely to their hearts. They see a supreme talent but not yet a regular match-winner; they see a nice lad but not yet a fully grown man, and they suspect a confident exterior hides a suspect temperament – fears that his recent two low scores in the LV County Championship against Hampshire will not have diminished. There is no better opportunity than an Ashes series to make a reputation good.

When Bell made 199 at Lord's against South Africa last summer, he showed that he has everything needed to succeed consistently, not just at Test level, because he has already shown he can do that, but in the kind of tough situations by which top batsmen measure themselves. His most significant fault is that, occasionally, he looks like he is enjoying a long net rather than playing the match situation. Indeed, a regular flaw of young English batsmen is that they are too preoccupied with technique (especially what are called trigger movements before the ball is bowled) and how things look, and not enough with reading the game situation: when to attack, when to dig in, when to take a risk and when to change the tempo of the game. If Bell can tailor his game better to suit the demands of the moment, he can become the player everyone has long expected him to be.

Bell was already named as the replacement batsman at Lord's, so technically there are no changes to England's squad for the third npower Test at Edgbaston that starts on Thursday, Monty Panesar and Stephen Harmison retaining their places. The selectors have decided against naming a spare batsman in case of injury, partly because there are now no injury concerns as there were with Pietersen before Lord's, and partly because there is no outstanding candidate.

The lack of obvious alternatives is one of the few clouds on the horizon for Miller, who said he had a 'strong idea' of where Bell will bat, but will not reveal anything until the morning of the match. With Bell returning and Ravi Bopara yet to look settled at number three, the Australians will view England's middle order as the point of weakness.

While the quality of this year's series has not matched that of four years ago, it is just as intriguing because of the flaws carried by each team. Another similarity to 2005 is concern over the state of the pitch. A violent thunderstorm disrupted preparations in the previous home series and recent low pressure over the Midlands has forced Steve Rouse to issue another early warning. This time he says his pitch is like 'jelly' and while it is usually unhealthy to take too much notice of groundsmen and their early prognostications, a slow surface would encourage England to retain faith with Graham Onions over both Harmison and Panesar.

Onions out-bowled Harmison in a County Championship match at Edgbaston earlier this year, is fully fit despite taking a blow to an elbow during his Ashes debut and would be unfortunate to be discarded after one admittedly modest showing. Panesar may come into the equation, but the slowness of any likely turn and his ineffectiveness at Cardiff is unlikely to persuade Andrew Strauss to change the balance of a winning team.

All that is based on the assumption that Andrew Flintoff will be fit to take his place in the starting line-up for Edgbaston. Miller said that the medics were continuing to manage the all-rounder's knee injury and that they are bullish about his prospects of playing. Missing Pietersen would be one thing; Flintoff, in his current mood, quite another.

No matter who is selected, it does not matter if they cannot get on the field to play. There is, perhaps, no more depressing place to be in the cricket world than Edgbaston on a day like yesterday, the eve of a Test match. Relentless rain sent the players indoors, and the Super Soppers, all five of them, outside and into overdrive, although they fought a losing battle against the elements. The forecast for the third npower Test match is unremittingly grim, an outlook that favours no one.

Certainly not England, who – although poor weather from here on in would enable them to have a better chance of holding on to their 1-0 lead – sense an opportunity to hammer home the advantage gained at Lord's. Despite Kevin Pietersen's absence, Andrew Strauss was in bullish, chipper mood at his press conference yesterday, happy to answer a query about the 'aura' of the Australia team by suggesting that, like the sunshine, it had disappeared.

This will come as no news to those who have watched Australia throughout a tour of England that has yet to bring any significant success. But it was not so much what Strauss said, more that he felt comfortable enough saying it, something that surely reflects the buoyant mood in the England dressing room. Strauss was not being deliberately provocative, he was simply answering a straight question in a straightforward manner, but he did not circle the question as previous captains might have been forced to do. 'It feels like we are playing against any other team,' he said.

Just like any other team is exactly what Australia have not been over the past two decades and the England captain's comments are sure to touch a nerve. Ricky Ponting finds himself in the unaccustomed position of having to come from behind and there is an unusual amount of speculation about the Australia team. 'It means we must be doing something right,' said Strauss. Quite so.

England have one decision to make for the start of the Test now that Ian Bell has been confirmed – in what could well be a defining month for him – at number four, and Monty Panesar has been given his marching orders because of the rain. Stephen Harmison, still to confirm or deny retirement rumours, is likely to miss out to allow Graham Onions the chance to present the seam at a surface that must have some residual moisture.

There is more uncertainty surrounding Australia, which is why England want as much play as possible over the next five days. Mitchell Johnson is struggling badly but may still retain the faith of the Australian selectors, while Brett Lee is not fit enough to warrant selection. Things will become much clearer over the next five days for Australia: if Lee becomes available and Johnson either bowls himself out of contention for good, or indeed finds some form, they can look forward to finishing the summer a good deal stronger than they started it.

Australia's default position after a defeat is usually to show faith, and Ponting has hinted strongly throughout the week that Johnson will play. There must be a temptation, though, to go for Stuart Clark, who acts as something of a lucky charm for the Australians – they have won 17 of the 22 Tests he has played. Clark for Peter Siddle would also offer Ponting some control with the new ball, and allow Johnson to step back from the pressures of leading the attack.

What neither captain doubted yesterday was the importance of the game. In 2005, Edgbaston was deliberately placed as a key Test match, Old Trafford following hard on its heels. It is no less important this time around, something Strauss was quick to acknowledge when he called it the 'hardest' Test of the summer. By that he means strategically the most important, with Headingley looming after a three-day break and not much chance for a beaten side to recover.

The England players enjoy Edgbaston more than any other ground because of the fervent, patriotic support. Ponting has been taken aback by the nature of some of the reaction, media and public, so far this summer, and should steel himself for a particularly rough ride over the next five days. He needs only 25 runs, though, to overhaul Allan Border's record for the number of runs by an Australian in Test cricket, and will hope, if not for veneration, then for something approaching appreciation should he get there.

He has never given the impression that he is a cricketer who gives more than a passing nod to personal milestones and he knows that defeat here would virtually consign him to becoming only the second Australia captain to lose two Ashes series in England. To prevent that, Ponting needs time that the weather here may not allow, and a better performance from his bowlers.

With all the talk of auras found and lost, there is no doubt that the one player on either side with an aura right now is Andrew Flintoff. Strauss confirmed he will be fit to play, barring last-minute problems. He was also asked how far he should protect the all-rounder. Rightly, he said that a player who makes himself available must expect his share of the workload. In any case, watching his stunning performance at Lord's, how bad can it be?

Day 1, Thursday 30 July

Close of play: Australia 126 for 1

The Edgbaston crowd is noted for its partisanship, but what they needed yesterday was patience, and plenty of it. At least when play finally got underway after six hours' waiting, it was patience rewarded as Australia responded to a late injury to Brad Haddin, the wicket-keeper, and what could have been a tricky two-hour session, in committed and aggressive fashion.

Heavy morning showers topped up the already high water table, so that despite the afternoon sunshine, the umpires deemed conditions unfit for play until five o'clock. There may be criticism of the Edgbaston authorities in some quarters, but Steve Rouse, the groundsman, and his team had worked through the night to get the ground in a playable state and they deserve some sympathy and credit.

If the outfield remained damp and muddy in areas, the pitch itself defied Rouse's pessimistic prognostications. It is a beauty, offering decent carry, and Australia took full advantage, rattling along at four runs per over in a session that brought 22 boundaries. With bad weather forecast at the weekend, Ricky Ponting will be looking to push on quickly on the second day.

Australia's swift progress was not so much pre-planned, though, more a result of England's shortcomings, since there were far too many opportunities to score offered by an attack that Andrew Strauss resisted the temptation to tinker with after the Lord's Test. Graham Onions had a chastening three overs and faces an early test of his mettle on the second day, when he needs to show that he can offer the captain some control.

Onions, though, was not the only culprit. The pace attack as a whole was inconsistent: Andrew Flintoff was unable to recreate the spirit of Lord's, James Anderson's inswinger was working but his outswinger not, and Stuart Broad was ineffective. It was a strangely subdued performance, Graeme Swann the honourable exception. Swann was given just a couple of exploratory overs, but he might have had Shane Watson leg-before, sweeping, with his second ball and then did get Simon Katich, pulling but missing a straight ball, with his sixth.

In a roll-call of great Australian opening partnerships, Katich and Watson will not figure, the former being a middle-order batsman by trade and inclination, the latter an all-rounder who has never batted higher in Test cricket than number six before, but who was answering a distress call. In the circumstances, their opening offering of 85 was particularly impressive.

Watson is a strong, uncomplicated player who does not so much caress the ball as clout it. He stands tall at the crease and moves in orthodox fashion forward or back according to length, quite the opposite of the man he replaced. He drove strongly down the ground when given the opportunity and pulled and cut whenever England erred short. When Flintoff tested him with the short ball, and a word or two of Lancastrian greeting, Watson smiled back. Freddie didn't seem to like that, and liked it less when Watson nudged him when running through for a single.

Three of the Australian selectors – David Boon, Andrew Hilditch and Jamie Cox – are former opening batsmen and so it seems strange that Australia are having to make do at the top of the order. Phillip Hughes's omission came as a surprise, then, both the manner of the announcement and the rationale behind it. This Ashes series has become something of a Twitter battleground, with commentators vying for popularity, but Hughes trumped them all by announcing his own demotion on his site, PH408, on the morning of the game. It will not be long before batsmen and bowlers are twittering from the crease: 'Freddie bowling fast, ducked another bouncer, LOL.'

Only last week, Ponting said that Hughes needed just a half-hour at the crease to find his best form, but now the man hailed as a genius and who came to England with a Test average of 69 found himself omitted for an all-rounder who had opened just six times in first-class cricket, with an average of 4.67. Hughes will come again, but his rather upbeat tweet ('will be supporting the guys') hides no doubt a crushing disappointment.

Ultimately the decision to omit Hughes was because of the poor form of Mitchell Johnson. His inclusion suggested that Ponting retains faith in his left-armer, but Watson's selection was as much about bolstering the attack, should Johnson's struggles continue, as it was about Hughes's poor form.

It was a decision that paid off, as did Ponting's choice to bat first, which cannot have been straightforward. He was faced with what might have been described as batting conditions but a bowling situation: a nice-looking pitch but a juicy two-hour session, the kind that bowlers love and batsmen find difficult. Did the demons of 2005 sway him? In the end, he made the right choice and walking off unbeaten, having passed 20,000 runs in first-class cricket with his first boundary, he can be well pleased with his contribution.

There was an uncanny echo of 2005 before the start of play when Australia lost one of their key men to injury. For Glenn McGrath read Haddin, who broke the ring finger of his left hand just moments before the start, but after the captains had handed over their team sheets. Australia were forced to go cap in hand to England and ask permission for the team to be changed. Strauss would have been within his rights to insist that Haddin played, but common sense prevailed. It is not the ideal way to earn your baggy green, but Graham Manou has joined an exclusive club.

Day 2, Friday 31 July

Close of play: Australia 263; England 116 for 2

If Australia had appeared to rediscover if not their aura then certainly some swagger on the first day, then the events of the second confirmed the way the tide has been flowing since Cardiff. Whereas their batsmen took up a proprietorial air at the crease on the first day, yesterday they signed up to the shortest of leases, losing nine wickets for 137 runs in a little under three hours.

In a way, Andrew Strauss had begun the reversal by unexpectedly giving Graham Onions the opening over of the day, which produced two wickets, and the England captain was the dominating presence throughout the afternoon. Playing with an enviable mixture of freedom and simplicity, he passed fifty for the 33rd time in Tests, his sights now set on loftier targets. When bad light was offered with 19 overs remaining in the day, he was undefeated on 64, England's deficit 147.

Strauss will have been delighted with the day, although his exacting standards had not been met at the fag end of Australia's innings, when the last two wickets added sixty precious runs. That, a couple of dropped catches, one by Andrew Flintoff and one, much simpler, by Ravi Bopara, and an indifferent performance with the ball again from Stuart Broad were the only clouds on an otherwise bright day for England.

Strauss's was a reassuring presence at the crease, the more so since his opening partner, Alastair Cook, edged his fourth ball to give Graham Manou his first catch in Test cricket and Bopara played a half-hearted defensive stroke just after tea to squander a decent start. The former could learn from Strauss's flawless judgement outside off stump, the latter from his concentration.

When Bopara played on to Ben Hilfenhaus, Ian Bell's moment had arrived once again. Although he was subdued at the start, he went into double figures with a thunderous six off Nathan Hauritz, a message perhaps that his days of submission to Australia are over, more likely a stroke of liberation now that his tormentor Shane Warne is not playing. Bell looked in good order generally but ought to have been given out leg-before to Mitchell Johnson on 18 – Rudi Koertzen looking for doubt where none existed. Bell then rubbed salt into the left-armer's wounds, leaning into a silky drive for four two balls later.

Johnson's tour is not improving, wicketless again and now a member of the Primary Club after his first-ball nought during a staggering opening session that was resonant of the first morning of the 1997 Ashes Test at Edgbaston when Australia were reduced to rubble. England took seven wickets in the first two hours, a session book-ended by two spells of sublime bowling from Onions and James Anderson. Onions began the day with wickets from his first two balls, and Anderson completed the session with four wickets in 13 deliveries, as Australia's batsmen showed little aptitude against the swinging ball. Why the ball had suddenly started to swing is anybody's guess. Maybe the lacquer had come off the ball, maybe the outfield was drier than the day before but, whatever the reason, bowling at Australia, anybody, is a different proposition when the ball moves in the air.

Anderson is a different animal, too, when the stars are in alignment and conditions suit. He can be one of the most destructive swing bowlers in the world, the movement often late and wicked, produced from a barely decipherable tilt of the wrist. Onions's success was more of a shock simply because of the immediacy of his success and the way Australia had dealt brutally with his three modest overs the day before.

Strauss's decision, therefore, to give Onions the first over was a masterstroke. Normal captaincy rules dictate that you start the session with your likeliest bowlers, who on the previous day's form would have been Flintoff and Anderson. But Strauss ignored Anderson's claims and showed very public faith in Onions (although he did begin the day with three fielders on the boundary). He was rewarded immediately, when the bowler skidded one through Shane Watson's defence with the first ball of the morning.

The Edgbaston crowd had barely settled into their seats, and indeed some had not yet entered the ground, when Onions found himself on a hat-trick. Mike Hussey had marched to the middle in double quick time, as if he had been expecting the worst, and then was marching back at an even more furious pace next ball, as he left a straight delivery for the second time in consecutive Tests that crashed into his off-stump.

Onions continued to ask questions, although Ricky Ponting stole his thunder momentarily when he went past Allan Border with a clipped three to become Australia's leading run-scorer in Test cricket, a feat properly acknowledged by crowd and batsman. When he miscued a pull over mid-on it was clear that Ponting had been surprised by Onions's pace off the pitch, and, surprised again, he attempted to pull a short ball from outside off stump and edged through to Matt Prior.

Now it was Anderson's turn. Michael Clarke missed an inswinger, and was unluckily adjudged leg-before with the ball doing too much; Marcus North drove airily, whereupon Prior launched himself to his left and pouched a stunning one-hander; Johnson left his first ball alone only to see it swing back and crash into his pads; and Manou, the debutant who walked onto the ground to chants of 'who are ya?', was opened up in classic fashion as Anderson moved wide on the crease.

This last was a beautiful piece of bowling and fully demonstrated the Lancastrian's mastery of the art of swing bowling. He had set up Manou with a number of outswingers from close to the stumps, which the batsman had left alone. Now Anderson jumped wide, so spearing the ball in towards the stumps. The batsman aimed to mid-on, the ball ghosted past the outside edge and Manou was gone, stumps splayed. Peter Siddle completed Anderson's haul just after lunch, his first five-wicket bag in Ashes Tests. The swagger now belonged to England.

Day 3, Saturday 1 August

No play possible

Steve Rouse, the Edgbaston groundsman, hasn't seen much of home sweet home lately. He and his team worked around the clock – seven hours of hard yakka while the rest of the world slept – to get the ground fit for play before the first day, but there was nothing they could do yesterday as the rain came down forcing the whole day to be abandoned, not a ball bowled.

By 2.40 pm the ground was a lake, and umpires Rudi Koertzen and Aleem Dar took the sensible option to send the players home for the day. Five sessions of play have been lost over the first three days and with more rain forecast on Monday, it may be that a result is beyond either team here, and England will go to Headingley with their lead intact.

When England do resume they will do so on 116 for 2 after a heartening 56-run stand between Andrew Strauss (64 not out) and Ian Bell (26 not out). Andy Flower, the England team director, was quick to point out how quickly things can change and sounded upbeat about his side's chances of victory.

'You can see how quickly things can happen in a game, so a result is definitely possible,' he said. 'Whether or not that happens, we'll have to see how well both sides play. But if we can get 70 overs in [on Sunday], we still have to bat well to get a lead. It's up to us to bat well and see how far ahead we can get.' The forecast is for sunny intervals for day four and light rain on Monday.

In the absence of any cricket, it was a struggle to find ways to amuse oneself. A posse of England players gathered in what was the old dining room, huddled around a card table, chips piled high. Poker is the game of choice for England's players right now, the size of the chips reflecting changing times. We used to play for matchsticks.

Shane Watson, Australia's makeshift opener, reckoned 500 was the most popular card game in the Australian dressing room, although he admitted to not playing because he didn't understand the rules. He looks a thoroughly uncomplicated bloke, does Watson, something reflected in his stand-up-and-hit-'em batting.

As for commentators on a rainy day? Bumble twittered, Beefy harrumphed and Warney and his teeth dazzled. Warne has been a terrific addition to the commentary box, great knowledge combined with earthy opinion, all offered in a voice fashioned from a thousand fags, endless bottles of booze and late-night card rooms. Bumble's obsession with twittering is remarkable, since he didn't know what Twitter was until our producer, Paul King, put him up to it on the first day of the series. Now he's besotted with it.

As for me? Five hundred words. Not exactly Cardus, but whaddya expect on a day like this?

Day 4, Sunday 2 August

Close of play: Australia 263 and 88 for 2; England 376

When, in two matches' time, Andrew Flintoff begins to reflect on his Test career, Birmingham will hold many fond memories.

It was here four years ago that he gave his most compelling all-round performance as an England cricketer and it was here, against the West Indies, that he scored his highest Test score. One sniff of the Edgbaston air is all it takes.

Yesterday he did not quite reach those heights, but his first significant contribution with the bat since Mohali last winter helped to secure England's position from which they can push for what would be a remarkable last-day victory. He hit 11 boundaries in an innings of 74, the boundary count significant since his running between the wickets betrayed the increasingly fragile state of his knee. Just four overs with the new ball confirmed his problems.

England will need Flintoff the bowler on the final day, just as they needed Flintoff the batsman yesterday, because the pitch is still good and Australia will need to bat only the best part of two sessions to make the game safe. If nothing else, Flintoff galvanises the crowd and late in the day, the atmosphere was as febrile as ever off the pitch, some of which spilt over into the middle.

Australia had reduced their deficit to 25 by the close. They lost two wickets in doing so, Simon Katich working across Graham Onions's probing line and edging behind, and Ricky Ponting, disgracefully booed to the crease again, bemused by a beautifully flighted off-spinner from Graeme Swann, one that curled, spun out of Mitchell Johnson's follow-through marks and ghosted through the Australian captain's forward push.

After Swann breached his defences, Ponting stood for an age at the crease, as if unable to comprehend how swiftly things had turned against his team. At that point it was possible to imagine a bundle of wickets falling, especially when Mike Hussey, on a king pair, edged his first ball onto his thigh pad, the ball ballooning in the air and landing just short of Onions's desperate dive in his follow-through. Australia are nothing if not resilient, though, and Hussey and Shane Watson did well to repel England's surge.

With so much time lost to rain and bad light, it is remarkable that England are contemplating victory at all. But from the second morning onwards the force has been with them, a belief reinforced in the last two sessions yesterday. Flintoff was the dominating presence in an afternoon session that brought 157 runs and saw England re-assert their authority. He shared partnerships of 89 with Matt Prior, who again played beautifully, and 52 with Stuart Broad and such was his evident disappointment when Nathan Hauritz surprised him with one that turned and bounced onto his gloves, that he was surely eyeing his first three-figure score since Trent Bridge four years ago.

He will be disappointed that he did not get a hundred, but once again it was a contribution that helped change the momentum of the day. England were 168 for 5 when Flintoff came to the crease, the crowd subdued, Australia bowling well and harbouring hopes of a first-innings lead. By the time he was out, England had a lead of 46, the crowd had come alive and only one team could possibly win the game.

Given that Flintoff has taken a 5-0 hammering at the hands of Australia, it is difficult to argue that he has the same kind of psychological hold over Australia as Ian Botham had, but put Edgbaston, Australia and Flintoff together, and sparks can fly. When he launched Hauritz into the stand to bring the scores level, and then smashed a sweep for four the next ball to take England into the lead, the Hollies Stand had become raucous and possibilities seemed endless.

Broad does not yet have Flintoff's ability to shape events, but he will hope to step into Flintoff's shoes after the end of this series, and, taking his cue from Flintoff, he showed that his batting at least will not suffer in comparison. Standing tall and refusing to be cowed when Australia came over all chatty, he breezed along to a half-century in only 62 balls, giving his team renewed momentum. With a contribution from Graeme Swann that increased Australia's irritation, England stretched their lead beyond what had seemed possible at lunch.

Australia will regret how they bowled at Flintoff at the start of his innings when, as if to order, they served up a number of delicious half-volleys for his delectation. Shane Watson, ignored until the 65th over by Ricky Ponting, was the worst offender, bowling in a manner that suggested his all-rounder status is in serious danger. Peter Siddle was equally wasteful so that the Australian captain, once again, had a limited attack at his disposal.

This was puzzling because Australia's bowling had showed some improvement in the morning session, Ben Hilfenhaus, who finished with four wickets, leading the way with a marathon 14-over stint either side of lunch, and Mitchell Johnson, cheered to the rafters by England's supporters when given the ball, at last rediscovering his menace.

Ridiculously, the crowd were forced to sit for an hour before any cricket was played. There were damp patches around the square, for sure, but nothing that ought to have prevented play immediately, another example of the game taking its paying supporters for granted. When play began, it did so on a pitch that had greened up overnight and under heavy clouds that held the promise of riches for Australia's seam attack.

It was Hilfenhaus who got the first two wickets of the morning, Andrew Strauss looking for room to cut where none existed, and Paul Collingwood lured into a fatal drive. Ian Bell played crisply for his half-century, driving with authority and pleasingly robust in defence, until Johnson darted one back into his pads. On another indifferent day for Australia, Johnson's improved form was a solitary shaft of light.

Day 5, Monday 3 August

Close of play: Australia 263 and 375 for 5; England 376

In the end, the best part of two days lost to bad light and rain, a pitch that remained, in the best Edgbaston traditions, something of a featherbed, and determined batting from Australia's middle order was enough to ensure that England's lead going to Headingley will be a slim one. The weather was the ultimate victor, because but for the disruptions a result would surely have been possible.

Whether it would have been Australia or England who would have won without the rain is open to debate, because when both teams accepted that a result was beyond them, the touring team's lead was a healthy one, 262 runs with five wickets in hand. All that can be said with certainty is that within the timeframe made available, it was England who made the running, a factor that should fill them with further belief as the series reaches its climax over the next three weeks.

England were never less than wholehearted yesterday, until the post-tea session when they had accepted their fate, but they lacked the magic ingredients that were necessary to dismiss good batsmen on a still-slow pitch. Andrew Flintoff's knee problems reduced his involvement to just 11 overs, during one over of which he took a bone-jarring tumble as he landed awkwardly on his left foot. He rose gingerly and refused to leave the field, hobbling thereafter in a manner that must raise concerns ahead of the fourth npower Test at Headingley.

With Flintoff largely redundant, the Hollies Stand, so boisterous normally, was graveyard quiet throughout the day. There was little else to stimulate them: no swing for James Anderson, and the sharp turn that had excited them and Graeme Swann the evening before failed to materialise. Swann did not bowl as well as he might during a day when expectations weighed heavily. His control of length was awry and Australia's batsmen snuffed out his threat effectively.

Australia's resilience has never been in question, and the four batsmen upon whom rested most responsibility – Mike Hussey, Shane Watson, Michael Clarke and Marcus North – all passed half-centuries, with Clarke becoming the first batsman to reach three figures with the final act of the match. As he approached his hundred he became uncertain for the first time, a delivery from Stuart Broad grazing his off stump on 92 and nicking a no-ball to slip on 96. Finally, he dispatched a long hop from Ravi Bopara to the square-leg fence to bring up his hundred, whereupon the captains called it quits.

For the most part the runs came easily in the final session, as England tired, but both North and Clarke had earned their easy passage by coming through a tough period earlier in the day. North was stubborn when he needed to be, but then flourished so that he would have beaten Clarke to three figures had Anderson not taken a brilliant diving catch in the gully off the improving Stuart Broad when he was four shy of the landmark. When Clarke and North came together, Australia were 161 for 4, the lead only 48 and the match will still very much alive, and it was their record fifth-wicket partnership for Australia at Edgbaston that slammed the door in England's face.

For Australia to lose they had to have one very bad session. But they lost only two wickets in the morning, none at all in the elongated afternoon session and one in the evening. Theirs will have been a nervous dressing room overnight and, therefore, they will take a great deal of heart from the ease with which they secured a draw. They will take added comfort from the sight of Brett Lee bowling at near maximum pace during the intervals.

Clarke played a very different innings from the sparkling one he played at Lord's, this one full of responsibility and more statesmanlike, provoking gibes from England's close fielders of 'job-seeking'. Clarke may harbour ambitions for the top job when Ricky Ponting retires, but for now he is happy to play his part as a batsman and what a player he is developing into – pleasing on the eye, chock-full of strokes and able to fashion his game according to the needs of the moment.

He gave only one chance, when he was on 38 and Australia's lead was 106. Andrew Strauss had turned to Bopara and Clarke, concentration perhaps momentarily misplaced, pulled the bowler straight at the England captain at short mid-wicket who spilt the catch.

There were times yesterday when Strauss's decision-making was puzzling. Anderson was ignored for the first hour of the day, which was strange, given his five-wicket haul in the first innings and the cloud cover that greeted the players at the start of the day. Instead, Flintoff and Graham Onions opened up, Flintoff, no doubt, to galvanise the crowd. He bowled a strong seven-over spell, roughing up Watson in the process, one particularly nasty bouncer hitting him on the elbow. Pain, but no physio called for.

There was even greater pain for Watson six balls after the drinks break when Anderson was finally brought into the attack. Bowling a full length, but absent of the kind of swing that makes him so dangerous, he tempted Watson to drive and feather an edge through to the wicket-keeper. Watson's inclusion as a batsman has been a success, two fifties justifying his selection, but there will be lingering disappointment that he could not convert either into something more substantial.

Hussey was playing nicely now, strong on the drive, firm in defence and looking every inch the determined cricketer he is. England's plan to Hussey is to probe around off-stump, the batsman's judgement occasionally unsound. Broad, the fifth bowler to be introduced and in need of wickets, did exactly that, and whereas Hussey's downfall in the first innings came when he offered no shot at a straight ball, now he played at one he should have left and edged behind. Australia went to lunch, effectively 59 for 4 and the game still open. Clarke and North put paid to that.

SCORECARD

ENGLAND v AUSTRALIA
At Edgbaston, Birmingham, on 30, 31 July, 1 (no play), 2, 3 August.
Result: **MATCH DRAWN**. Toss: Australia.

AUSTRALIA	First Innings	Runs	Mins	Balls	4/6
S.R.Watson	lbw b Onions	62	130	106	10
S.M.Katich	lbw b Swann	46	83	48	9
*R.T.Ponting	c Prior b Onions	38	88	47	5
M.E.K.Hussey	b Onions	0	1	1	–
M.J.Clarke	lbw b Anderson	29	94	55	4
M.J.North	c Prior b Anderson	12	63	49	1
†G.A.Manou	b Anderson	8	20	11	2
M.G.Johnson	lbw b Anderson	0	1	1	–
N.M.Hauritz	not out	20	78	50	1
P.M.Siddle	c Prior b Anderson	13	31	26	2
B.W.Hilfenhaus	c Swann b Onions	20	37	31	4
Extras (B 5, LB 7, W 2, NB 1)		15			
Total (70.4 overs; 319 mins)		**263**			

Fall of Wickets: 85-1 (Katich, 18.6 overs); 126-2 (Watson, 30.1 overs); 126-3 (Hussey, 30.2 overs); 163-4 (Ponting, 38.3 overs); 193-5 (Clarke, 49.4 overs); 202-6 (North, 51.4 overs); 202-7 (Johnson, 51.5 overs); 203-8 (Manou, 53.5 overs); 229-9 (Siddle, 61.5 overs); 263-10 (Hilfenhaus, 70.4 overs).

ENGLAND	Overs	Mdns	Runs	Wkts	Econ	Strike
Anderson	24	7	80	5	3.33	28.8
Flintoff	15	2	58	0	3.87	–
Onions	16.4	2	58	4	3.48	25.0
Broad	13	2	51	0	3.92	–
Swann	2	0	4	1	2.00	12.0

ENGLAND	First Innings	Runs	Mins	Balls	4/6
*A.J.Strauss	c Manou b Hilfenhaus	69	178	134	11
A.N.Cook	c Manou b Siddle	0	7	4	–
R.S.Bopara	b Hilfenhaus	23	70	54	4
I.R.Bell	lbw b Johnson	53	147	114	7/1
P.D.Collingwood	c Ponting b Hilfenhaus	13	27	22	3
†M.J.Prior	c sub (P.J.Hughes) b Siddle	41	100	59	6
A.Flintoff	c Clarke b Hauritz	74	116	79	10/1
S.C.J.Broad	c and b Siddle	55	92	64	9
G.P.Swann	c North b Johnson	24	23	20	5
J.M.Anderson	c Manou b Hilfenhaus	1	7	6	–
G.Onions	not out	2	20	14	–
Extras (B 2, LB 4, W 6, NB 9)		21			
Total (93.3 overs; 399 mins)		**376**			

Fall of Wickets: 2-1 (Cook, 1.4 overs); 60-2 (Bopara, 19.2 overs); 141-3 (Strauss; 44.1 overs); 159-4 (Collingwood, 50.5 overs); 168-5 (Bell, 55.6 overs); 257-6 (Prior, 71.3 overs); 309-7 (Flintoff, 80.4 overs); 348-8 (Swann, 87.3 overs); 355-9 (Anderson, 88.6 overs); 376-10 (Broad, 93.3 overs).

AUSTRALIA	Overs	Mdns	Runs	Wkts	Econ	Strike
Hilfenhaus	30	7	109	4	3.63	45.0
Siddle	21.3	3	89	3	4.14	43.0
Hauritz	18	2	57	1	3.17	108.0
Johnson	21	1	92	2	4.38	63.0
Watson	3	0	23	0	7.67	–

Third Test, Birmingham 30 July–3 August

AUSTRALIA	Second Innings	Runs	Mins	Balls	4/6
S.R.Watson	c Prior b Anderson	53	183	114	9
S.M.Katich	c Prior b Onions	26	55	47	2
*R.T.Ponting	b Swann	5	6	7	–
M.E.K.Hussey	c Prior b Broad	64	154	130	13
M.J.Clarke	not out	103	281	192	14
M.J.North	c Anderson b Broad	96	208	159	15
†G.A.Manou	not out	13	39	28	1
M.G.Johnson					
N.M.Hauritz					
P.M.Siddle					
B.W.Hilfenhaus					
Extras (B 4, LB 6, W 2, NB 3)		15			
Total (5 wkts; 112.2 overs; 466 mins)		**375**			

Fall of Wickets: 47-1 (Katich, 13.2 overs); 52-2 (Ponting, 14.6 overs); 137-3 (Watson, 43.6 overs); 161-4 (Hussey, 52.6 overs); 346-5 (North, 103.1 overs).

ENGLAND	Overs	Mdns	Runs	Wkts	Econ	Strike
Anderson	21	8	47	1	2.24	126.0
Flintoff	15	0	35	0	2.33	–
Onions	19	3	74	1	3.89	114.0
Swann	31	4	119	1	3.84	186.0
Broad	16	2	38	2	2.38	48.0
Bopara	8.2	1	44	0	5.28	–
Collingwood	2	0	8	0	4.00	–

Umpires: Aleem Dar (*Pakistan*) (57) and R.E.Koertzen (*South Africa*) (100). Referee: J.J.Crowe (*New Zealand*) (36). Man of the Match: M.J.Clarke.

Birmingham Test Facts:

- James Anderson's 5 for 80 was his first Ashes five-wicket haul, and his seventh in all Test matches.

- 1 August was the first entire day's play to be lost in England in an Ashes series since 19 June 1997.

- Michael Clarke's 103 not out in the second innings was his fourth Ashes century and the 12th of his Test career; he was the last man to score hundreds in successive Ashes Tests, in 2006–07.

- Michael Clarke and Marcus North's fifth-wicket partnership of 183 was the highest by Australia at Edgbaston.

Fourth Test, Leeds

7–9 August

The Build-up

Undeterred by the furore that greeted the selection of Darren Pattinson last year at Headingley, the England selectors have searched again beyond those whose games have been fashioned within these shores. Jonathan Trott, the uncapped Warwickshire batsman who was born, raised and produced in South Africa, becomes the latest lucky cricketer to experience that Ashes feeling.

At the time, the selectors argued that Pattinson had been picked on form and there is no doubt that Trott, 28, is the in-form batsman in county cricket. Three championship centuries, runs at a tick under 100 a time and a magnificent Twenty20 campaign have brought his name again to the attention of the selectors – one of whom is his county's director of cricket, Ashley Giles – after a brief experiment in two Twenty20 internationals against West Indies in 2007.

Trott has been included in a 14-man squad, with Monty Panesar omitted (conditions at Headingley could not be less spin-friendly), Stephen Harmison retained and Ryan Sidebottom named for the first time this summer. That it is anybody's guess which of the three has the best chance of playing speaks volumes for the selection conundrums that face England before the fourth npower Test starts on Friday 7 August.

Trott has been added to the squad because of the increasing

concern over Andrew Flintoff's knee. The all-rounder was restricted to 11 overs on the final day of the drawn third Test at Edgbaston, although no doubt he could have bowled more had circumstances dictated. Ricky Ponting was accused on Tuesday of firing the first Headingley shots by saying post-Test that Flintoff looked increasingly sore as the game progressed.

Flintoff struggling? Really? It was a surprise, then, upon meeting the Queen at Lord's, that Ponting wasn't accused of a republican conspiracy. Yesterday Andy Flower, the team director, acknowledged the fact while adding that Flintoff was 'bullish' about playing, but reiterated that everyone in the team knew of the contingency plans should the 31-year-old be deemed too big a risk.

Flower was happy to talk around those contingency plans without revealing their exact nature. 'If Fred can't play, then Trott is an option at six and we balance the bowling thereafter,' he said. 'We might still go in with [Stuart] Broad at seven, [Graeme] Swann at eight and three bowlers. We trust our top six to score the bulk of the runs, the onus is on the others to take 20 wickets.' In the latter scenario, Harmison, fitness permitting, would be a straight swap for Flintoff.

Harmison, though, is not fully fit, suffering from blisters in Durham's last LV County Championship match, which is why Sidebottom has been drafted in. He is bowling well for Nottinghamshire, has vast experience of conditions in Leeds, where he learnt his cricket, and, crucially, gives England another swing-bowling option from a different angle. He is deemed to be fitter and in better form than he was throughout the Caribbean tour last winter, when he looked a shadow of the bowler who burst back into the team in 2007 after a long absence.

The biggest puzzle will be if the medics decide that Flintoff cannot get through and, in his absence, conditions dictate a stiffening of the batting, with Trott at number six, Matt Prior returning to seven and four bowlers. In that scenario, four bowlers should mean the best four bowlers and Broad's form should come under scrutiny. He bowled his best spell of the series at the fag end of the Edgbaston match, but he has taken only six wickets in three Tests, each costing more than 50 runs (identical figures, as it happens, to Swann).

Flower was quick to defend his young all-rounder. 'He has handled everything that international cricket has thrown at him incredibly well since he came in,' he said of the 23-year-old. 'I think he is a fantastic young cricketer now and he is going to be even better as he progresses and as the team progresses. Yes, he has had a quiet series with the ball, but he has chipped in every now and then, and he is part of that five-man attack, and that attack has to dovetail a little.

'I am very happy with Stuart. He is a great competitor who is learning about bowling and batting in the best arena possible. His innings at Edgbaston was impressive and the last time we played at Headingley, he played an even more impressive knock against the South Africans.'

Everything, really, hinges on Flintoff. If he is fit, the likelihood is that, despite taking only three wickets on the final day in Birmingham, England will be loath to tinker and will play the same team. If he is not fit, a suspect pitch would improve Trott's chances, cloud cover would improve Sidebottom's and neither of the above would represent Harmison's best chance of one last crack at Australia before he, too, heads off into the sunset.

Beyond the specific matters of selection policy, and even the outcome of the Ashes, there are broader issues that affect us all in cricket and we cannot forget about the broader picture.

Imagine this scenario: a great sportsman, popular beyond measure, has announced his retirement and has only two matches left before he rides off into a lucrative sunset. His career and reputation are made, but he knows that the earning potential from his last two games, if things go well and his team win the series and with it his sport's greatest prize, is immeasurable. There is one small problem: he's injured.

How badly injured, he doesn't really know. He knows, though, that he is hurting but that he has to play in the last two games. Just has to. Cortisone, legal, frequently administered and a wonderful masking agent for pain, won't do the trick since there is a limit to how much of it the body can quite properly cope with, and he's already had five injections this year. So he asks around. Takes something, anything, and plays his last two matches.

Far-fetched? Fanciful? Thankfully yes, since cricket historically has not had a problem with drugs, either performance-enhancing ones or those designed to mask injuries. Isn't it good to be able to say that? A team game presumably presents more barriers to drug abuse than an individual sport, so isn't it good to know that England and Australia are giving us their real selves this summer, rather than a Frankensteinian version created by those who would distort through drug-induced means?

Readers of the sport section of *The Times* might have been forgiven for wondering what kind of people professional sport produces, with Dwain Chambers, the convicted doper, grinning back at us while telling us of his plans for Usain Bolt, and the 'Bath three' – Michael Lipman, Andrew Higgins and Alex Crockett – following their colleagues, Matt Stevens and Justin Harrison, into shame-faced oblivion. Let's not even get started on cycling. Or swimming.

Cricket can claim no leasehold on the higher moral ground, for sure. The match-fixing story of the 1990s was one of the worst to befall any sport, there being no greater deception on the paying public than athletes deliberately trying to lose, give their wickets away or leak easy runs. Sport is an unwritten contract between those who play and those who watch and, for the most part in the 1990s, it was a contract broken by the performers.

But, for a leading sport, there have been relatively few drug scandals in cricket. Shane Warne, now of *The Times*, was sent home from the World Cup in 2003 when hydrochlorothiazide and amiloride, diuretics or classic masking agents (take your pick) were found in his bloodstream. Warne had made a rapid recovery from a shoulder injury to play in the tournament and, when tested and found guilty, was banned for a year, although Dick Pound, head of the World Anti-Doping Agency (WADA) at the time, argued it should have been more.

Three years later, Shoaib Akhtar and Mohammad Asif were also banned for testing positive for nandrolone, the first time cricketers had been found abusing banned steroids. Other than that, most drug offences have been of the recreational type, Ed Giddins arguing that his drink had been spiked with cocaine and myriad others (Ian Botham, Phil Tufnell, Stephen Fleming among them) pleading guilty to taking a puff or two of marijuana. Overall, though, in a period when drugs have decimated other sports, cricket has been relatively unscathed.

In part this is because of a laudable attempt by the authorities to treat the issue seriously. The International Cricket Council signed up to WADA's stringent regulations in 2006, a prerequisite, of course, to becoming an Olympic sport and, in England, a necessary first step to guarantee government funding. So whereas, ridiculously, the 1990s was a period where county cricketers were tested but international cricketers not, now international players know that if they transgress they will be found out.

All has been going swimmingly until this week, when the Board of Control for Cricket in India (BCCI) backed a number of high-profile Indian players who have said they will not comply with the 'whereabouts' clause. This clause stipulates that cricketers of a high enough international ranking must give WADA notification of their whereabouts for one hour each day with three months' notice for a period of a year. If the athlete is not where he says he will be, he gets one strike. Three strikes and gone.

India's cricketers – and they are not alone – have expressed reservations because of the potential security threat to the likes of Sachin Tendulkar, who is known to want to keep his movements secretive, and because of the gross invasion of privacy such stringent testing implies. There are fears more generally that such a system will penalise those who are administratively inefficient rather than those who are guilty. These are legitimate concerns.

Ultimately, though, it is a price that cricketers may have to pay if they want their sport to remain clean and, more importantly, to be perceived to be clean. While the chief executive of the players' union, Tim May, accepts the practical difficulties in adopting the system, he should also recall his comments three years ago when he warned that the increasingly punishing schedule may force players to start abusing drugs.

'You only have to look at the doping record in baseball to see that recovery, not enhanced power, is the motivation for most drug abuse. The more we push the players, the more they may start to look at options,' he said.

May's nod in baseball's direction is relevant, it being another sport whose reputation is in shreds. And for cricketers who want their achievements to be recognised rather than mired in suspicion, they should think about someone like Mark McGwire, the former Major League home run record-holder who has yet to be inducted into the Hall of Fame because of doubts about his drug-taking. By refusing to answer questions about steroid abuse in front of a congressional hearing, McGwire cast doubt on his own record and that of everyone else of that era.

Integrity is at the heart of sport, which is why match-fixing was cricket's most serious crisis and why snuffing out the drugs threat, even if the threat is a vague one and the methods seem unnecessarily draconian, is vital. In the scenario painted earlier, Freddie would, of course, say 'no'. To the 'whereabouts' clause and drugs testing in general, the rest of cricket should say 'yes'.

The conclusion seems inescapable: if Headingley Carnegie produces a result – and this is highly likely given that since 1981 there have been only two draws here – then to the winners will go the Ashes.

This is self-evident in England's case, as a win would give them an unassailable lead in the series and spark off the kind of jingoism that would make Edgbaston's booing of Ricky Ponting look tame indeed. But if Australia turn things around in Leeds, it is difficult to see how Andrew Strauss's team will bounce back and bowl them out twice on what is traditionally the flattest pitch of them all at The Oval. The next five days, then, shape as the most pivotal of the summer.

Looming over the contest, like the pair of giant cranes at the soon-to-be-redeveloped Kirkstall Lane End, is Andrew Flintoff, who bowled in the nets for 40 minutes yesterday without looking anywhere near full fitness. The heaviest of knee braces and the glummest of moods would have done little to reassure his supporters. On the eve of the Test match, as England pondered their options, it was looking increasingly unlikely that he would play.

Strauss said yesterday that the selectors would make a hard-nosed, unemotional decision and they, not Flintoff, would make the call, although clearly they will take notice of his mood and wishes. Headingley was always going to be the biggest hurdle for him, coming so hard on the heels of Edgbaston, and it would be an amazing turnaround from his final-day lassitude there if he is fit to take the new ball at the start of the Test. And even if he can bowl a decent first spell, can he guarantee a second and a third? And what about the following four days? It would be a gamble too far.

Contrary to popular opinion, Flintoff did not have cortisone injections before the last Test. Rather, he had lubricant injections, which are nothing like as dangerous. He could endure more of them, but each day of action brings greater swelling, nature's way of demanding some rest. One last hurrah at The Oval beckons.

In Flintoff's likely absence, England have some awkward decisions to make. Do they stiffen their batting, bringing in Jonathan Trott – who incidentally was parading around in a shirt with both his initials and England number on – so changing the policy of the summer at a stroke? This would send out defensive signals, a battening-down-of-the-hatches, pro-tecting-the-lead kind of a decision, which would go against Strauss's well-aired pronouncements about how attacking cricket is the best way of beating Australia.

If Trott plays, does that mean Stuart Broad is vulnerable in a four-man attack? Broad has struggled to be an effective fourth seamer this summer, never mind third, and if he does miss out, who should be England's third pace bowler, Stephen Harmison or Ryan Sidebottom?

Better, with all this uncertainty, to make just one change – a straight swap of Harmison for Flintoff. It would be the posi-tive thing to do; it would necessitate less upheaval and allow for a like-for-like replacement with the ball. In any event, debutants in Ashes series have rarely fared that well in recent times, and Broad would be as likely to make his mark with the bat as Trott.

If Strauss was faced with the trickiest decisions of the eve of Test, Ponting has his own problem to deal with, namely Brett Lee. The fast bowler has been bullish about his fitness in the build-up to this game but, as with Flintoff, time has not been on his side, and there have been previous occasions when Lee has failed to deliver on fitness. It would be a huge risk, in a four-man attack, to play him without any cricket under his belt, and he, too, may have to wait until The Oval, when an outing against England Lions the weekend before the fifth Test should have proved beneficial.

Injuries notwithstanding, both teams went about their business with impressive efficiency the day before the Test, but the flaws are difficult to hide. This has been a well-matched but modestly skilled contest so far. England are fretting over Flintoff, a middle order that is suspect and a bowling attack that appears increasingly toothless if conditions go friendly; Australia need a result pitch, but know that their batsmen have looked vulnerable to the moving ball, and their bowlers have been unable to locate a length on a consistent basis.

With bare concrete substructures protruding at the Kirkstall Lane End, Headingley is a ground turning its attentions at last to the future and away from the past. Ponting could have been forgiven for hoping for a better tomorrow, too, because his immediate future as Australian captain could depend on what happens over the next five days. To lose the Ashes once in England is just about acceptable, to lose them twice, well, that could be seen as unnecessarily careless.

Such knowledge is likely to sharpen his game and his punting instincts. Ponting has an outstanding record as a batsman at Leeds, scoring hundreds in both his appearances there, including his first as a Test match player. He could do with some runs now, the well having run dry since Cardiff. Is the pressure of leading a modest team taking its toll? He has looked fidgety, for sure, since his opening salvo of this series, but he is often a poor starter and champions tend to raise their game when it matters.

What is certain is that his reaction to the moment will be a positive one and Australia's team selection is likely to reflect the captain's mood, even if he has no formal vote on selection. Nathan Hauritz has performed better than his reputation suggested he would, but he is likely to be less effective here than anywhere else and it takes a leap of faith to imagine him as a match-winner. Expect Australia to play four seamers, with Marcus North accepting the spin bowling duties and Stuart Clark finally getting the chance to show how badly Australia have missed his control.

Day 1, Friday 7 August

Close of play: England 102; Australia 196 for 4

Throughout the summer, Andrew Strauss has been making bullish noises about his team's ability to cope without their alpha males, Andrew Flintoff and Kevin Pietersen. The hypothetical became a reality as England took to the field for the first time in nearly six years without either. The response was not so much a statement of independence as a cry for help, Australia bowling out England for their lowest Ashes total at Leeds in a hundred years and finishing the day in credit, if not quite, yet, in clover.

Before the start of this game, England were effectively five good days from regaining the Ashes. But so disastrously did things go for the first two sessions, from the early news of Flintoff's withdrawal, to Matt Prior's pre-match back spasm – which required a last-minute injection – to the thoroughly inept batting, and bowling that, in its own way, was just as poor, that it will take a remarkable turnaround if England are to go to The Oval with their lead intact.

This pantomime summer has seen Ricky Ponting cast as the ugly sister to Strauss's Cinderella, booed every time he has appeared on stage. He was booed thunderously to the crease by a certain section of the crowd again, more a raspberry to inter-fering administrators than any hatred of Ponting, and was booed off the stage as well, but by the time he departed leg-before to Stuart Broad, his team were already 38 to the good.

Ponting played the innings of the day, even if he was helped by an English attack that was far more accommodating than the clowns on the Western Terrace. The bowling was short and often wide, as if to order, so that Ponting was able to showcase to his detractors the cutting and pulling at which he is just about the best in the business. He shared in a century partnership with Shane Watson, the fifty-and-out man, which consolidated his team's earlier gains. A lead of 150 or more should prove enough.

In the wake of a first-innings batting performance so woeful that only two batsmen made double figures, questions will no doubt be asked about England's team selection after Flintoff's withdrawal. But those who argue for the extra batsman – selecting

Jonathan Trott at the expense of Broad – will be aiming arrows at the wrong target. England were collectively awful, so much so that one player could hardly have made that much difference, and Broad was the best bowler in the last session, snaring Mike Hussey as well as Ponting.

Once Prior had recovered from his back spasm, England made one change, Stephen Harmison replacing Flintoff. It was a show of faith in the five specialist batsmen, but they suffered a failure of nerve, technique and planning. All five were caught in the arc between wicket-keeper and gully, four of them for single-figure scores, as Australia bowled the kind of full, prob-ing length that was beyond England later in the day.

Certainly this proved to be a decent toss to lose for Ponting, the ball swinging consistently in the morning and darting off a dry surface like a chased buck, but that is nothing less than you would expect at this most capricious of grounds. Headingley demands craftsman-like disciplines – playing tightly around off stump, not driving anything other than half volleys, not chasing anything too wide – and these were ignored.

Credit, though, to Australia who, by replacing Nathan Hauritz with Stuart Clark, got their selections spot on and set about consolidating the momentum they believed had come their way at Edgbaston with their best bowling performance of the summer.

Although Peter Siddle took five wickets, the first and the last four, Clark was central to Australia's improvement. His absence until now has been something of a surprise because he has always seemed ideally suited to English conditions. There have been whispers that he has lost a little of his nip, but given the movement on offer, the premium was on accuracy not pace. A ten-over spell of exquisite medium-pace swing and cut either side of lunch brought him four maidens, three wickets – Alastair Cook and Paul Collingwood pushing forward and Broad clipping to short square leg – and England just 18 runs. He applied the tourniquet that Australia have been missing throughout the summer.

Clark's pressure from one end brought benefits at the other as England's middle order was exposed again. Ravi Bopara, looking increasingly out of his depth at number three, hung his bat out limply to Ben Hilfenhaus and was caught in the gully, while Ian Bell failed to get his glove out of the way of a rip-snorting bouncer from the improving Mitchell Johnson. Only Matt Prior, stranded on 37, stood tall.

It was the most difficult day that Andrew Strauss has had as captain, with a fire alarm going off at the team hotel at an unsociable hour and the shenanigans surrounding Prior's late fitness test. The key for captains who are opening batsmen is to be able to put the worries to one side when the first ball comes down. But there was so much going on before the start of play, so many decisions to make and such a short space of time once the toss had been put back by ten minutes, that it would have been near impossible.

So when Hilfenhaus bowled a perfect first delivery – the kind that a left-hander dreads above all (full length and swinging back into the pads) – the surprise was not that Strauss missed it but that Billy Bowden did not raise the crooked finger. It was plumb. A mighty reprieve, then, but the captain's mind was clearly elsewhere, and he wafted 16 balls later at a wide ball from Siddle, Marcus North pouching a stunner at slip. It was a bad start for Strauss on a day when his Ashes dreams may have turned to dust.

Day 2, Saturday 8 August

Close of play: England 102 and 82 for 5; Australia 445

Summoning up all kinds of likely omens before the match, Stewart Regan, Yorkshire's chief executive, called upon the ghosts of 1977 (Geoff Boycott's hundredth hundred) and 1981 (Botham's Ashes) as rallying cries. The 2009 Headingley Ashes will be memorable all right, and may well go down in folklore as those other famous occasions have, but for entirely the wrong reasons if you are an England supporter.

Had Marcus North clung on to Matt Prior's edged drive off the last delivery of the day, the ball bursting through his fingers to register a rare Australian mistake in the game, Ricky Ponting could well have claimed the extra half-hour and tried to finish off England in two days. Given the way England had batted, the umpires would have had no option but to grant Australia's captain his wish. Two days! You can beat England in quicker time than it takes to listen to the cycle of the Nibelungen.

For a while, when Andrew Strauss and Alastair Cook were accumulating an opening stand of 58, there was hope that England's first innings was simply a seedy memory best forgotten. But then the excellent Ben Hilfenhaus nipped one back, off a frayed surface, into the England captain's pads, securing a leg-before decision that only partially made up for the one he should have had against Strauss with the first ball of the match, and then four more wickets fell for 20 runs in just 43 balls in an astonishing end to the second day.

England's middle order looks shot, the first wicket a horrible precursor to the inevitable collapse. Ravi Bopara's shocking series continued when he was half forward to Hilfenhaus's first ball. He might have got a thin 'un, but it looked out enough in real time and it looks as though Australia have his measure. Ian Bell survived the hat-trick ball – just – but didn't last long thereafter, softened up by Mitchell Johnson before edging a length ball to second slip. Bell, as ever, gives off the impression of a batsman made up of less than the sum of his parts.

Paul Collingwood's series has declined ever since his memorable rearguard action in Cardiff. But, really, the mental exertion of Cardiff has less to do with Collingwood's meagre returns than the absence of Kevin Pietersen. Not only do they bat well together, Collingwood, like others, sails along beautifully in Pietersen's slipstream, but when asked to make headway all of his own, sends out distress signals almost immediately.

He was worked over beautifully by Johnson, who sent the batsman across his crease with a number of wide, going wider, deliveries. Collingwood, across to off stump to cover the angle, had no answer to the ball that then darted back late. Plumb in front.

Then Cook, whose 30 from 84 balls was painful to behold, albeit necessary in the circumstances, fenced at Johnson, and edged through to Haddin. And that was just about that, with Matt Prior and James Anderson clinging on grimly to take the game into the third day.

Australia extended their overnight lead of 94 to a better-than-expected 343, thanks to more orthodox defence and strokeplay from North and a little more dazzle from Michael Clarke. North's second hundred of the series (remember, he also fell just short of another at Edgbaston) was more evidence that the Australian system is incapable of producing duffers; even their so-called humdrum cricketers provide a lesson in self-reliance, discipline and productivity. He reached his hundred with a slog-swept six off Graeme Swann, not unlike how one imagined Kenny Barrington might have gone to his hundred, careful replaced by carefree on one glorious moment.

Clarke was the hare to North's greyhound, forever in front, never likely to be caught. He waltzed to his half-century in just 78 balls, particularly severe through the covers on James Anderson, who now was limping courtesy of a quick single to get off the mark the day before. England's management insisted that Anderson was fully fit, although the evidence did not suggest so.

Clarke looked destined for his third hundred of the series, when Graham Onions, strangely short and ineffective here when conditions ought to suit, swung a yorker into Clarke's boots. The ball might have been sneaking down, but it looked close enough. The partnership of 152 with North was not quite as big as at Edgbaston but it was just as damaging, even more so because it gave the tail a licence to create some havoc at the end of the innings, which Stuart Clark happily accepted, three sixes coming in a classic tail-ender's innings.

Stuart Broad was the most successful of England's bowlers, finishing with six wickets, an achievement he celebrated in the fashion of Glenn McGrath, holding the cherry up to the crowd. He kept going, which is an attribute not to be sniffed at, but, really, that was about the sum of it. Catches came, not in the slip cordon, but at deep square-leg as Australia played with abandon. Broad's crankiness – at umpires, batsmen and sometimes his own team – is about all he has in common with the Narromine Nagger right now.

And so England slunk off at the end of a day during which the much-talked-about momentum of the series had changed utterly. Before the game, the buzz was of the Western Terrace and their, at times, unseemly support for England. The administrators seemed beside themselves to work out how best to prevent them from offering jingoistic support. They needn't have bothered: England's pale imitation of a Test-class side has done the job perfectly for them this game. They left the field to silence.

Day 3, Sunday 9 August

Close of play: England 102 and 263; Australia 445

There was fun and frolics to be had on the final morning at Headingley, but the last laugh belonged to Australia. This was a crushing victory and the final flourish provided by Stuart Broad and Graeme Swann had no more effect on the punishment dished out than the student who flicks a 'V' at the headmaster once his back is turned.

This was the stuff of men against boys. The fresh-faced, almost angelic-looking Broad and the cheeky chappie Swann throwing the blade with abandon and grinning cheerfully, as Australia became ever more ragged, provided some amusement, even solace for a short time. But when Graham Onions was bowled to give Australia their victory by an innings and 80 runs, the realisation dawned quickly that England had been so utterly outplayed, that the momentum shift was so complete, that the hopes of a revival at The Oval are nothing more than mere fancy.

If, before the series began, England had been offered a level scoreline before the final Test, they might well have taken it. But that hypothetical fails to take into consideration the way that Australia are peaking just at the time that England are imploding. As Andrew Strauss was answering searching questions in the wake of his biggest defeat as captain, Ricky Ponting was playing daddy with his baby on the outfield. There is no question who is under pressure now.

Perhaps England supporters can draw some comfort from what happened after the last time Strauss felt as badly as he will this morning. England did not manage to win any Tests in the Caribbean after they were bowled out for 51 in Jamaica last winter, but Strauss emitted such a palpable sense of calm then that rapid improvement quickly followed. Strauss, you sense, is a good man for a crisis.

And a crisis is exactly what England are in right now. Kevin Pietersen is injured; Andrew Flintoff is disgruntled, having been spurned at Headingley, and the middle order have gone AWOL, just 16 runs between Ravi Bopara, Ian Bell and Paul Collingwood for six times out at Headingley. Against that, Australia are coming to the boil nicely, five wickets for Mitchell Johnson confirming his return to form, and Brett Lee fully fit again, to judge from his post-match bowling out on the Headingley pitch as his colleagues began their celebrations.

It is impossible to imagine anything other than the Ashes returning to Australia, but England, of course, cannot be thinking like that and must work out how to approach the final match at The Oval. The first thing they must do is ensure that the groundsman, Bill Gordon, produces a result pitch. This will go against the instinct and inclinations of The Oval authorities, but nevertheless the call must be made.

Flintoff is next on the agenda. Clearly, given what he put himself through at Lord's and Edgbaston and the injections he has had throughout the summer, he will be feeling sore in more ways than one. He will feel that he has been rejected, and some careful man-management will be required from Strauss and Andy Flower, the team director, to ensure that he is properly focused ahead of what will be his final Test.

In his post-match press conference, Strauss said that Flintoff had to be able to fulfil his duties as a bowler to be considered. In other words, he has to be able to bowl three spells in the day, which Strauss, presumably under medical advice, felt he would not be able to do at Headingley. Even so, Flintoff's presence at number seven would have stiffened a flimsy-looking line-up, and the player himself is surely the best judge of whether he can get through a match or not. If he says he is fit at The Oval, he must play.

As must all the batsmen bar Strauss when the round of county games begins on Tuesday. Bopara and Alastair Cook can make their way to Lord's, where Essex play Middlesex, and Collingwood and Bell to Old Trafford and Trent Bridge respectively. There is a world of difference between county and Test cricket, but every batsman feels better with runs under his belt and once the games are finished on Friday, there will still be three full days off before the squad meets again for The Oval.

Bopara's place is under the biggest threat. Unlucky he may have been in the second innings, but his first-innings dismissal suggested a man from whom confidence is rapidly draining away. Flower, who knows him best, must make a judgement call as to whether he is mentally shot. If so, he should be withdrawn from the firing line. If not, he must play and bat at number three, as any demotion down the order would provide Australia with too much ammunition in the field.

The lack of batting alternatives is truly frightening and Jonathan Trott's selection at Headingley a desperate indictment of a system that is not producing enough home-grown players of quality – and a curious one, too, given his non-selection for the Lions match against Australia in July. The two highest run-scorers in county cricket are Marcus Trescothick and Mark Ramprakash, but the former does not want to play and the latter's time, seven years after his last Test appearance, has surely come and gone. If an alternative number three is needed, better to go with Rob Key or Owais Shah.

It is hard to imagine that any changes would improve a desperate situation. Anything that smacks of panic would probably make things worse. Far better to retain faith in players who, until the start of the Headingley game, had their noses in front and hope that the wild fluctuations in fortunes that have characterised this series work to England's advantage again.

It is, to be sure, not much of a plan: a result pitch, Flintoff returning with a script ready-made and written, one hopes, in the stars, and blind faith shown in a Pietersen-lite middle order. England were so bad over the last three days that, surely, they cannot be so again. Can they?

The Aftermath

Andrew Flintoff had declared himself fit and ready to play on the eve of the fourth npower Test at Headingley, only for the England management to refuse to gamble with the all-rounder's fitness. A devastated Flintoff was not seen at the ground throughout the match. Flintoff will see his surgeon and England will be desperate for him to play in the deciding match at The Oval, which starts on 20 August. It would be Flintoff's last match before he retires from Test cricket.

Andrew 'Chubby' Chandler, Flintoff's agent, revealed the extent of the all-rounder's disappointment. 'I've seen a few disappointed sportsmen over the last couple of months, but I've never seen anybody as low as Flintoff was on Thursday night when he was told he would not be selected.

'He told them that he was fit enough to get through, that he felt no different to how he felt at Edgbaston and that he could get through and do his bit. They didn't want him. He was prepared to do whatever it takes, was prepared to put whatever needed to be put into his knee. The whole point of announcing his retirement when he did was to clear his head and prepare to do whatever needed to be done to play the final Test matches of his career. He just didn't see it coming. He wanted to play and they didn't want him, and he didn't see that coming at all.'

Although Andrew Strauss, the England captain, said clearly before the match that the decision on Flintoff's availability would be taken by himself and Andy Flower, the team director, it was widely assumed after watching the all-rounder's final net session on the day before the game, that the decision to leave him out was taken in conjunction with Flintoff and his medical advisers. Clearly not.

England will insist that Flintoff's selection was too much of a gamble and that the decision to leave him out was a strong one. How much better it would have been if they had shown a similar amount of strength at the beginning of the season over Flintoff's and Kevin Pietersen's participation in the Indian Premier League. Pietersen carried an injury into that tournament and Flintoff was injured during it, so that England played the most important days of the summer without either.

Questions will now be asked about the wisdom of leaving England's talismanic all-rounder out of such a critical fixture. If he was certain that he could get through, was the risk not worth taking? Given the way he batted at Edgbaston, he would certainly have stiffened a batting line-up that failed miserably at Headingley, given Strauss some much-needed control with the ball, and provided the balance so clearly missing.

Chandler insists that the adrenalin would have helped the all-rounder to beat the pain barrier at Headingley, as it did at Lord's. 'What they didn't take into account during Thursday's practice was that there was no adrenalin. That was why he looked as though he was struggling so much and why he became so much worse on the final day at Edgbaston, when it was clear the game could not be won. He was hurting at Lord's but the adrenalin got him through. It would have got him through this week as well. His presence would certainly have lifted the crowd and the team, because without him they don't have much inspiration.'

As England begin the process of recovering from the heavy defeat at Headingley, and begin to work out their options for The Oval, Flintoff will see his surgeon. Between them they will work out a medium-term prognosis that is likely to include the possibility of further surgery after the last Test and then a long rehabilitation programme before he begins his new career as a one-day player only.

He now has 11 days to get fit for The Oval Test, the final one of his outstanding career – providing England want him, of course. Even if he does play, the events at Leeds mean that the fairy-tale ending he so craves looks an increasingly distant dream.

SCORECARD

ENGLAND v AUSTRALIA
At Headingley, Leeds, on 7, 8, 9 August.
Result: **AUSTRALIA won by an innings and 80 runs.** Toss: England.

ENGLAND	First Innings	Runs	Mins	Balls	4/6
*A.J.Strauss	c North b Siddle	3	16	17	–
A.N.Cook	c Clarke b Clark	30	104	65	3
R.S.Bopara	c Hussey b Hilfenhaus	1	10	6	–
I.R.Bell	c Haddin b Johnson	8	40	26	2
P.D.Collingwood	c Ponting b Clark	0	13	5	–
†M.J.Prior	not out	37	76	43	5
S.C.J.Broad	c Katich b Clark	3	13	12	–
G.P.Swann	c Clarke b Siddle	0	21	15	–
S.J.Harmison	c Haddin b Siddle	0	8	6	–
J.M.Anderson	c Haddin b Siddle	3	7	10	–
G.Onions	c Katich b Siddle	0	1	1	–
Extras (B 5, LB 8, W 1, NB 3)		17			
Total (33.5 overs; 163 mins)		**102**			

Fall of Wickets: 11-1 (Strauss, 3.6 overs); 16-2 (Bopara, 6.4 overs); 39-3 (Bell, 15.3 overs); 42-4 (Collingwood, 18.3 overs); 63-5 (Cook, 22.2 overs); 72-6 (Broad, 24.5 overs); 92-7 (Swann, 29.4 overs); 98-8 (Harmison, 31.4 overs); 102-9 (Anderson, 33.4 overs); 102-10 (Onions, 33.5 overs).

AUSTRALIA	Overs	Mdns	Runs	Wkts	Econ	Strike
Hilfenhaus	7	0	20	1	2.86	42.0
Siddle	9.5	0	21	5	2.14	11.8
Johnson	7	0	30	1	4.29	42.0
Clark	10	4	18	3	1.80	20.0

Fourth Test, Leeds 7–9 August

AUSTRALIA	First Innings	Runs	Mins	Balls	4/6
S.R.Watson	lbw b Onions	51	121	67	9
S.M.Katich	c Bopara b Harmison	0	9	4	–
*R.T.Ponting	lbw b Broad	78	119	101	12/1
M.E.K.Hussey	lbw b Broad	10	16	10	2
M.J.Clarke	lbw b Onions	93	193	138	13
M.J.North	c Anderson b Broad	110	321	206	13/1
†B.J.Haddin	c Bell b Harmison	14	25	23	1
M.G.Johnson	c Bopara b Broad	27	70	53	5
P.M.Siddle	b Broad	0	1	1	–
S.R.Clark	b Broad	32	24	22	1/3
B.W.Hilfenhaus	not out	0	6	3	–
Extras (B 9, LB 14, W 4, NB 3)		30			
Total (104.1 overs; 463 mins)		**445**			

Fall of Wickets: 14-1 (Katich, 1.4 overs); 133-2 (Watson, 27.3 overs); 140-3 (Ponting, 28.6 overs); 151-4 (Hussey, 30.3 overs); 303-5 (Clarke, 72.6 overs); 323-6 (Haddin, 80.2 overs); 393-7 (Johnson, 96.3 overs); 394-8 (Siddle, 96.6 overs); 440-9 (Clark, 102.5 overs); 445-10 (North, 104.1 overs).

ENGLAND	Overs	Mdns	Runs	Wkts	Econ	Strike
Anderson	18	3	89	0	4.94	–
Harmison	23	4	98	2	4.26	69.0
Onions	22	5	80	2	3.64	66.0
Broad	25.1	6	91	6	3.62	25.2
Swann	16	4	64	0	4.00	–

ENGLAND	Second Innings	Runs	Mins	Balls	4/6
*A.J.Strauss	lbw b Hilfenhaus	32	97	78	4
A.N.Cook	c Haddin b Johnson	30	136	84	4
R.S.Bopara	lbw b Hilfenhaus	0	1	1	–
I.R.Bell	c Ponting b Johnson	3	12	12	–
P.D.Collingwood	lbw b Johnson	4	10	10	–
J.M.Anderson	c Ponting b Hilfenhaus	4	20	10	1
†M.J.Prior	c Haddin b Hilfenhaus	22	40	29	3
S.C.J.Broad	c Watson b Siddle	61	95	49	10
G.P.Swann	c Haddin b Johnson	62	100	72	7/1
S.J.Harmison	not out	19	43	28	4
G.Onions	b Johnson	0	8	7	–
Extras (B 5, LB 5, W 5, NB 11)		26			
Total (61.3 overs; 275 mins)		**263**			

Fall of Wickets: 58-1 (Strauss, 22.4 overs); 58-2 (Bopara, 22.5 overs); 67-3 (Bell, 25.5 overs); 74-4 (Collingwood, 27.6 overs); 78-5 (Cook, 29.6 overs); 86-6 (Anderson, 32.3 overs); 120-7 (Prior, 38.6 overs); 228-8 (Broad, 51.3 overs); 259-9 (Swann, 59.2 overs); 263-10 (Onions, 61.3 overs).

AUSTRALIA	Overs	Mdns	Runs	Wkts	Econ	Strike
Hilfenhaus	19	2	60	4	3.16	28.5
Siddle	12	2	50	1	4.17	72.0
Clark	11	1	74	0	6.73	–
Johnson	19.3	3	69	5	3.54	23.4

Umpires: Asad Rauf (*Pakistan*) (25) and B.F.Bowden (*New Zealand*) (55).
Referee: R.S.Madugalle (*Sri Lanka*) (110). Man of the Match: M.J.North.

Leeds Test Facts:

- England's first innings score of 102 was their lowest Ashes total at Headingley since they made 87 in 1909, and their lowest in any Ashes Test since they made 79 at Brisbane in 2002–03.

- Peter Siddle's five for 21 in the first innings was his first five-wicket haul in the Ashes and his second (and best) in all Test matches.

- Marcus North's 110 was his second century of the series and his third in all Test matches.

- Stuart Broad's six for 91 was his first five-wicket haul in Ashes Tests and his second (and best) in all Test matches.

- Stuart Broad and Graeme Swann's eighth-wicket partnership of 108 was England's highest for that wicket at Headingley in the Ashes since 1981 when Ian Bothan and Graham Dilley added 117.

- Mitchell Johnson's five for 69 was his first five-wicket haul in the Ashes and his third in all Test matches.

- England's loss by an innings and 80 runs was their worst in an Ashes Test since they lost by an innings and 99 runs at Melbourne in 2006–07, and their 12th worst innings defeat in all Ashes Tests.

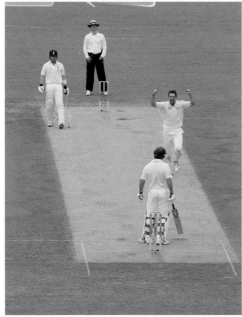

Ben Hilfenhaus celebrates as Andrew Strauss is caught behind after getting England off to a steady start in the crucial deciding Test.

Ian Bell faced up to a barrage of short-pitched bowling, especially from Mitchell Johnson, on his way to making 72.

Jonathan Trott is brilliantly run out by Simon Katich to bring to an end a promising first knock for England.

After Australia had got through the morning unscathed, suddenly everything was about to change in one of the most remarkable sessions of cricket in Ashes history.

73 for 1: Stuart Broad celebrates as Shane Watson is LBW.

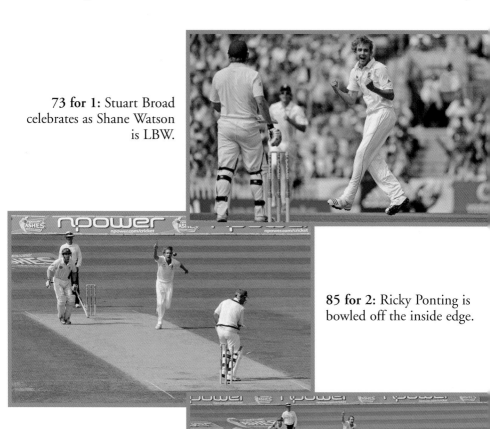

85 for 2: Ricky Ponting is bowled off the inside edge.

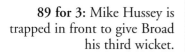

89 for 3: Mike Hussey is trapped in front to give Broad his third wicket.

93 for 4: Michael Clarke's firmly hit drive finds only the hands of Jonathan Trott, who took a great low catch at short extra-cover.

108 for 5: Marcus North's fine inside edge is not spotted, as umpire Asad Rauf gives him out LBW to Graeme Swann.

109 for 6: Simon Katich's resolute resistance is finally broken as Alastair Cook has the easiest of catches at short leg.

111 for 7: Stuart Broad bowls Brad Haddin to complete a magnificent five-for in the afternoon session.

131 for 8: Matt Prior celebrates catching out Mitchell Johnson just before the tea break. England went in strong favourites to retain the Ashes.

Marcus North immediately showed how much Australia had erred in failing to select a spinner when he picked up the wicket of Alastair Cook for just nine in the second innings.

Graeme Swann's aggressive innings of 63 helped put England out of reach. Throughout the series, he scored his runs at a faster rate than anyone.

Jonathan Trott proves the doubters wrong by becoming the first England player to score a century on debut since Graham Thorpe in 1993.

He might not have taken a wicket in the second innings, but Andrew Flintoff's direct hit to run out Ricky Ponting was a turning point as England looked to secure the Ashes.

A brilliant stumping by Matt Prior sent Marcus North back to the pavilion.

Paul Collingwood takes the catch in the slips off Stephen Harmison as Mitchell Johnson falls. Harmison would pick up three late wickets to leave England on the brink of victory.

Mike Hussey is last out as the England fielders celebrate Alastair Cook's catch off Graeme Swann: the Ashes are England's.

The England team get ready to lift the urn, after regaining the Ashes with a 2-1 series victory.

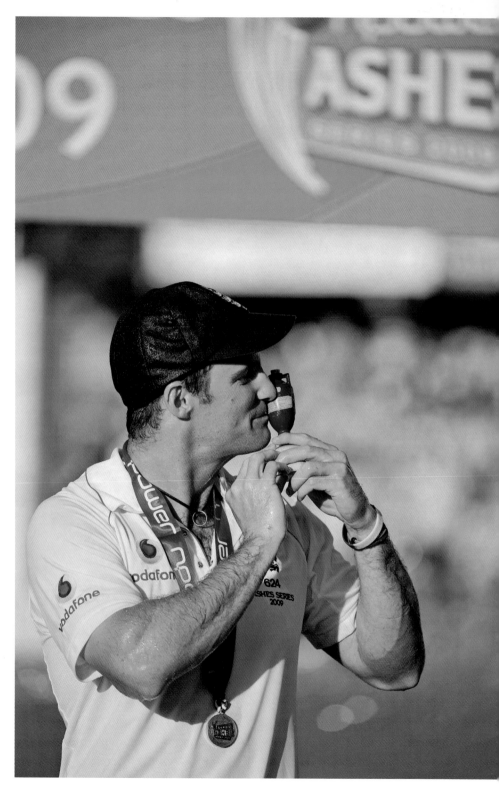

England's captain and man of the series, Andrew Strauss, kisses the urn. His calm authority and excellent form with the bat were key factors in England's success.

Fifth Test, The Oval

20–23 August

The Build-up

'A little aura goes a long way,' wrote one of our most celebrated sports writers at Headingley. 'A boomerang' that came back to hit Andrew Strauss 'straight between the eyes', wrote another of the England captain's premature judgement before the match at Edgbaston. Strauss will have plenty of time to ponder the nature of Australian and English cricket this week and the still yawning gap that exists between them.

The gulf is nothing to do with talent or aura. Both teams are equally matched in the former, especially when Andrew Flintoff and Kevin Pietersen are available to England, and, no, this Australian team do not carry the same aura as previous visitors to these shores. But one thing this Australian team have in common with their predecessors is toughness, a soul-deep toughness that, at the critical moment, befriended them again while deserting their opponents.

The winning moments in sport always come down to toughness in the end. Whether you are standing over an eight-foot put to become the oldest man to win the Open; whether you are five miles from Marathon glory in stinking 40-degree heat; whether you are running up in front of a stationary ball with just the goalkeeper to beat, and millions watching on television; or whether, with the ball darting this way and that, you simply have to find the kind of length so easily located when the brain is not sending distressed messages to the fingertips.

Toughness might be easily separated into two kinds, physical and mental, although there is a strong degree of overlap between the two. This week, in Justin Langer's leaked plans and Australia's performance under pressure, and in the pre-match tough-guy talk of Stuart Broad and England's performance under pressure, both camps gave us a compelling insight into the nature of their cricketers and the systems that produce them.

The real insight from Langer came not from his deciphering of the England's technical shortcomings but of their temperaments. Leave Bopara to strut alone, said Langer, not that the right-hander has stuck around long enough to know whether the advice has been well received. Wear down James Anderson and he'll go quiet. England's players will stare a lot but retreat very quickly. 'It is just how they are built,' he said. 'They love being comfortable.'

Langer is suitably embarrassed about the leaking of his plans, which came on the back of much showering of praise on county cricket, his paymaster, which, of course, produces all these 'pussies'. But didn't England do a splendid job of proving him right at Headingley? 'Aggressive batting, running and body language will soon have them staring at their bootlaces,' said Langer, and at every moment in the contest, which lasted just about until Ricky Ponting, that arch competitor, reacted to the early dismissal of Simon Katich in the only way a street fighter can, he was proved right.

Shortly before the Headingley Test, Stuart Broad showed how little he understands of the essence of Australia's competitive instinct when he had this to say about England's performance at Edgbaston. 'It has probably surprised them a little bit that we've shown we're quite a tough team,' he said. 'If someone stares at us and looks us in the eye, we all stare at them and look them back. It's quite a powerful thing if you are doing this sort of thing as a unit.'

Broad did not have a bad match at Leeds, taking six wickets and scoring a second innings half-century, but his wickets camouflaged what was, at best, an all-right bowling performance from him and a shocking one from the team. There was much staring at batsmen, whingeing at umpires, too, as they penalised him for 'hiding' the ball outside off stump, and even the odd bawling-out of a team-mate. But there was precious little consistency during the critical early stages of Australia's first innings and the showboating at the end of the game came when the pressure was well and truly off. Even so, Broad was the best of a bad bunch.

He is a promising young cricketer, but, listening to his comments, he misunderstands the true nature of mental toughness. Maybe other England players do, too. When the Ashes were won in 2005, many ascribed the win to England's toughness and their preparedness to 'stand up' to Australia, as they did *en masse* to Matthew Hayden in a famous contretemps at Edgbaston. The drubbing 18 months later was put down in some quarters to the absence of the *esprit de corps*.

Toughness has nothing to do with staring, sledging or ganging up on the opposition. It has everything to do with an ability to execute hard-won skills under maximum pressure. The Ashes were won in 2005 because England held their nerve and because a group of wonderfully skilled bowlers showcased their talents at crucial times. Australia were not outfought, they rarely are, but they were outplayed.

England have outplayed their opponents on occasions throughout this series, at Lord's and at Edgbaston. But Australia have never capitulated as England did at Headingley. They rarely do. England may yet prove Langer wrong about the 'it is how they are built' gibe, but one thing is certain – competing and producing under pressure is exactly how Australian cricketers are built. It is why they start favourites at The Oval.

To try to tip the balance back in favour of England, there is a lot of debate about which changes ought to be made to England's line-up for The Oval. In the 1989 Ashes series England used 29 players and lost 4-0; in 1993 they used 24 players and lost 4-1. The change of personnel not only made things worse, it made English cricket into a laughing stock. It was the kind of panic that Ricky Ponting smelt after Headingley when he was asked whether Mark Ramprakash should be recalled.

It would be a wonderful story, of course, for those of us who deal in stories. But the selectors' currency is not flights of fancy but fact and here are a few for those who think that Ramprakash, or Marcus Trescothick for that matter, should return at The Oval: Ramprakash is 39 years old and has not played Test cricket for seven years; when he last played, against New Zealand, he averaged 15 in five innings, and he has scored two Test hundreds in 52 matches. He has spent his time of late gorging himself, quite beautifully it must be said, in the second division of a modest competition. Phillip Hughes quite enjoyed the second division, too.

Trescothick has never scored a Test hundred against Australia, has not played for England since returning home with depression from the last Ashes tour and is – significant this – retired from international cricket. He did not rule out yesterday that he might change his mind if the selectors asked him, but he did not exactly jump at the opportunity either. 'I just don't know,' he said. 'I just don't know.' Not the kind of gung-ho attitude needed in this series decider.

In the same way that Jonathan Trott's selection was a startling admission of the failure of the English system to produce enough home-grown players of quality, so the selection of Ramprakash or Trescothick would highlight the bankruptcy of the LV County Championship in producing any credible contenders of the right age and ambition.

But, comes the cry, it's a one-off Test, a must-win Test. Isn't every Test a must-win game? The sooner we start approaching every game with that attitude, the better we may become. If they are the best men for the job, they were the best men for the job in Cardiff, too, but where were those voices advocating their selection then?

Mostly, they were salivating over the silky strokeplay of Ravi Bopara, who had just scored three consecutive centuries against the West Indies. That, by the way, is one more than Ramprakash scored in a decade of Test cricket.

With that debate about who should be selected for The Oval growing every day, it is time for the selectors to earn their keep. While the circus that surrounds English cricket has been going through one of its routine bouts of *The Generation Game*, picking players off the conveyor belt according to little more than whim and fancy, it is to be hoped that the selectors embraced a sense of calm and some common sense as they sat down to pick the squad for The Oval.

Trent Bridge was the venue, to fit in with Ashley Giles's other commitments, and it was deemed serious enough for Andrew Strauss to make his way to the Midlands to give his views, carrying as he does plenty of influence, if not a vote. This selection panel is watertight with its information, and the only leaks about their deliberations related to the lunch order: cheese sarnies and wedges with salsa dip.

A conservative order for a conservative bunch (although the salsa might keep supporters of Mark Ramprakash interested) it might be thought. Certainly this panel does not have a history of radical changes in direction and the only one expected now is the omission of Ravi Bopara.

Emerging teams – and England, despite disappearing up their own backsides in two and a half days at Headingley, are an emerging team with a relatively new captain and an inexperienced coach – rarely advance without the odd backward step. Ever since Strauss and Andy Flower took the helm seven months ago there have been only two serious blips in Test cricket, 51 all out in Jamaica and the Headingley rout. You wouldn't believe it from what has been said this week, but that is not a bad record.

Within that period, the batting, so much the focus of the

craziness since the fourth Test, has been a model of consistency. Other than at Headingley, where 102 represented about 200 short of parity, the lowest first innings score has been 376 at Edgbaston, followed by 377 against West Indies at Lord's, after which there have been two scores of 400 or more, three of 500-plus and one of 600.

This last came in Barbados, and how long ago that must seem for Ravi Bopara now. There is a fine line between confidence and cockiness, and when Bopara went through to a century in Bridgetown, celebrating in the manner of Usain Bolt, it was unclear which side of that line Bopara occupies, and whether the obvious presence of the latter hides an absence of the former. It is still unclear.

Which is why, unless Flower senses that the flame has been snuffed out completely by Australia's bowlers, the selectors should keep faith with Bopara. Selecting players is both an investment for the future and an excavating process. You keep digging until you find gold or hit something concrete, and they will find out more about Bopara over the next week than at any other time. Imagine the rich vein to be mined if he came through with a score.

If he is to be discarded – and one senses that his unbeaten half-century in the county championship as the selectors made their decision came too late to save him – one change to the batting is about all the selectors will countenance. As magnificent a story as it would be – and John Woodcock in *The Times* was right to place Mark Ramprakash's return within a romantic context – it is difficult to see the selectors tempting ridicule.

Either way, his return would present a problem for them: if

he plays, and does well, then legitimate questions would be asked of a selection panel that has ignored England's best-oiled run machine for years; if he does badly, they will be accused of caving in to media pressure, and not doing their job. Picking the best XI to win a match is the requirement, of course, but a bit of back-covering is likely. It may be that Ramprakash has matured mentally – who doesn't? – while retaining a remarkable fitness and appetite for runs. Just don't expect the selectors to want to find out.

If Ramprakash inhabits one extreme of the tried and tested scale, then Jonathan Trott occupies the other. Given that he was unlikely to play, his selection at Headingley was a poor piece of forward thinking, since the selectors will feel duty-bound to pick him now, especially as he scored another hundred during the week for Warwickshire. Trott is the likeliest replacement for Bopara, but, surely, this cannot be the game to blood a debutant, given all the uncertainties such a move would entail.

The hysteria and hype at The Oval will place a huge premium on temperament and the selectors cannot know how Trott will respond. They have more of a clue with Rob Key, who has been involved with the Lions team, in a leadership capacity, and therefore must be highly regarded by the selectors. Rumours of a spat with Flower during the World Twenty20 are unfounded and he is running into decent form at the right time. Duncan Fletcher, coach when Key was involved last against Australia, spoke highly recently of the batsman's temperament when last he toured there.

As for the bowling, expect Monty Panesar to come into the squad, but not to play. The Oval suits pace, bounce and spin, but not those who look to move the ball off the seam, so Stephen Harmison will be retained and may get the nod over Graham Onions and Ryan Sidebottom in the final eleven.

Possible England XIV: A.J.Strauss (capt), A.N.Cook, I.R.Bell, I.J.L.Trott, P.D.Collingwood, M.J.Prior, A.Flintoff, S.C.J.Broad, G.P.Swann, J.M.Anderson, S.J.Harmison, G.Onions, M.S.Panesar, R.J.Sidebottom.

One shocking performance, a media frenzy, much romantic speculation and five hours of deliberations at Trent Bridge have produced only one casualty. Ravi Bopara, who began the series aiming to make history as the first England batsman to score four consecutive Test hundreds, ends it consigned to history for the second time in his short international career.

Well, not exactly history, since Geoff Miller, the national selector, emphasised that Bopara remains on the selectors' radar for the near term. But there is no hiding the fact that he has failed the test for the second time since he made his debut in Sri Lanka in December 2007. His career graph so far is that of a cardiac-arrest victim being given the electric shock treatment, so extreme have been his peaks and troughs, and a half-century for Essex in their LV County Championship against Middlesex came too late to give him a further reprieve.

The Essex man is so highly regarded by Andy Flower, the England team director, that his demotion can only be a sign that Flower, who has seen him at close quarters for a number of years, believes Bopara to be mentally shot, his half-hearted first innings dismissal at Headingley the latest sign. If so, then the selectors have taken a humane decision.

But what should be resisted now is Bopara's rapid return in the winter. The England team should be hard to get in to, hard to get out of, and then, when dropped, doubly hard to get back into. If being axed carries no penalty for the likes of Bopara and Ian Bell, then players such as Owais Shah could justifiably complain of favouritism. Bopara has been found wanting. He needs time now to toughen up.

Jonathan Trott, then, will make his debut at The Oval in the biggest Test to be played in England since the Ashes were won for the first time in nearly 19 years in 2005. Preferred over Rob Key, but not Mark Ramprakash who was never in contention, this is a remarkable show of faith from the selectors in a man who has played only a couple of Twenty20 internationals so far and whose temperament for the big occasion is completely untested. It also smacks of poor planning.

Trott's timely hundred for Warwickshire before the team was selected bolstered his claims, although once the selectors had picked him for Headingley they would have felt duty bound to stick with him – a lesson perhaps that decisions should always be taken with half an eye on the future. Still, he is in cracking form for his county and carries a self-confidence characteristic of players born, raised and produced in South Africa. He is likely to bat at number four, although surely Paul Collingwood (why no county cricket for him this week, by the way?) should now take more responsibility, allowing Trott to come in at five.

If an Ashes series is supposed to be a battle of supremacy between the English system and the Australian system, a chance to boast that county cricket is superior to state cricket, that finger spin is superior to wrist spin, and blocking to dashing, then there should be some disquiet about Trott's promotion. The more the selectors pick players who have learnt their cricket abroad, then the contest becomes not one of English cricket versus Australian cricket but one of immigration policies.

Bell, also in the runs for Warwickshire since Headingley, will once again be promoted to number three, a position he has found about as comfortable as a badly sprung mattress. His average at first drop is a tick over 30, compared with a nudge under 40 overall, the numbers correlating with the feeling that he lacks the punch to thrive in that vital position. A part-Warwickshire middle order may raise questions about the impartiality of Ashley Giles's advice, or, if they fail, about his judgment of character since he sees them at close hand every day in the Warwickshire dressing room.

There were no other surprises in the squad of 14 who will go to The Oval, let us not forget, with a chance to regain the Ashes. With all the talk about the batting post-Headingley, it had been forgotten that the bowling was just as bad. James Anderson's hamstring twinge is not deemed bad enough to prevent his selection, but there is plenty of cover in any case with Graham Onions, Stephen Harmison and Ryan Sidebottom all in the squad.

Monty Panesar returns so that Andrew Strauss will have a balanced attack at his disposal should conditions dictate. The focus, though, will all be another player who missed out at Headingley and returns now. The bulletins on Andrew Flintoff's knee are positive enough that the selectors felt no need to include an extra batsman. Flintoff will play, then, despite the disquiet felt about his camp's post-Headingley pronouncements. Top-class players often bang on about their scriptwriters, and the all-rounder is no exception: the perfect ending is ready to be penned.

Are we allowed to disagree with our colleagues at *The Times*? Oh, very well then. This was Simon Barnes, the paper's celebrated chief sports writer, some weeks ago on one of his favourite topics, Freddie Flintoff: 'There are those who will tell you that Andrew Flintoff is not a great cricketer. Have no truck with such people.' Better look away now then, Simon.

Flintoff will bow out of Test cricket in the manner of a great cricketer this week, hosannas thrown in his path at every turn, but that is a very different thing from having achieved greatness. The hoopla surrounding his farewell will be a true and honest reflection of the place he occupies in the hearts of the majority of England supporters, and that really is the nature of the debate before us: how far can greatness be based on the fleeting things such as popularity, and how far on an analysis that puts him in context and pits his record and significance against the greats of the past?

If it is necessary to define greatness, rather than relying on something intuitive and from the gut, we could turn to Barnes again, who seems to have spent his life in search of it in the sporting arena. Of the nature of sporting greatness he has written: 'You look for someone who might achieve great things in sport. Napoleon would ask his generals, "Have you luck?" I ask of athletes, "have they Redgrave?" Redgrave is the ability to go beyond yourself. It is the ability to commit, day after day, to the goal of winning.'

Although this is a good starting point, it is too narrow a definition of greatness, and it doesn't necessarily help those individuals in a team sport, because there can be great players in losing teams. Brian Lara is a recent example. Winning alone takes no account of the extra-curricular qualities that Flintoff has in abundance, the ability to entertain, to draw in people and to change the mood of the moment with a single delivery or stroke that sets the crowd alight. Winning is empirical; the Flintoff question more theoretical.

So let us draw up a greatness ledger for Flintoff, for and against.

Is the manner in which a cricketer plays a prerequisite for greatness? Dennis Lillee would argue not, but most great cricketers have played the game in a certain spirit, not necessarily as set out in the preamble to the laws of the game, but a certain spirit nonetheless. Flintoff, without question, has done that. He has played with a smile, with respect for his opponents uppermost in his mind and with a permanent sense of adventure. The moment when he bent down to commiserate with Brett Lee after the Edgbaston match in 2005 was the iconic moment of the series and will be used down the ages when erroneous stories are told about how the modern game is a degenerate version of the past.

Certainly, Flintoff is the most popular English cricketer of the modern age – you could make a case for saying he is the most popular English cricketer since Denis Compton – and he is certainly the most popular sportsman in England today. After his drink-related episode on the Western Front at the start of the summer, he was cheered to the rafters the next time he walked out to bat. People identify with his bloke-next-door image, even though this is largely the product of spin, and they forgive him his foibles. More than that, they love him for them. Good old Fred!

He has a generosity of spirit equal to that of Sir Ian Botham, without the edge and bitterness that characterised Botham's great years. Flintoff comes across as warmer, and although these things are difficult to quantify, I reckon his popularity is more widespread than Botham's. Mothers across the land wouldn't mind Flintoff as a son-in-law; they'd be petrified of the thought of Botham taking their dearest up the aisle. Flintoff's popularity has drawn countless youngsters to the game. We are a country for ever in search of heroes, and Flintoff has provided us with one.

Nor can it be doubted that Flintoff is capable of great moments, great series and a great period even. His spell at Lord's this summer, which prompted Barnes's eulogy, was a spell of genuinely great fast bowling, during which he communicated with the crowd better than any England cricketer since Botham. He was a great cricketer in the Ashes series of 2005, when he bent a great team to his will, and between 2004 and 2005 his record is that of a great all-round cricketer: taking his wickets and scoring his runs at the kind of rate and average of which specialist batsmen and bowlers would be proud.

There is a but coming, though. Rather a few buts, actually.

The biggest – and *The Times'* chief sports writer will stop reading now if he hasn't already – is his record. Those damn statistics. Without exception in the modern game, greatness has been conferred on those with outstanding records in international cricket. The conferring of greatness must adhere to these strict guidelines out of respect for past heroes. Flintoff has a very good record, but not a great one. His bowling average is marginally higher than his batting average, and three five-wicket hauls and five Test hundreds speaks of a cricketer whose performances have fallen short of the very highest standards that great all-rounders should aim for.

It is almost as if, like Prufrock, Flintoff saw the moment of his greatness flicker and was afraid. He had a chance to embrace greatness after 2005, but instead the latter half of his Test career has been characterised by injury, drunken escapades and a disastrous tilt at the captaincy. For him, 2005 was the beginning of the end, rather than the start of something special, as it could have been. Until this summer, he had neither taken a five-for nor scored a hundred in any first-class game since that 2005 series. Instead, he has been content to embrace celebrity: chat shows, fly-by-night friends, a charitable foundation and at times an embarrassing exploitation of his position.

He was given an opportunity to alter perceptions of himself and his team, but he retreated into something more comfortable, more forgiving. How significant a cricketer was he, then, for England? Not as significant as Nasser Hussain or Michael Vaughan, it could be argued. Has he helped to change the culture of the team? Has he helped to transform them into world beaters? Clearly not. England were a workaday outfit when he first appeared, winning occasional big series as in Flintoff's debut summer against South Africa. They are still a mid-ranking team (fifth in the world) winning important series only occasionally.

If Flintoff had played every Test match since debut, he would have played 142 Tests, rather than the 79 with which he will finish. In a little more than a decade, then, he has played in marginally over half the Test matches that England have played, mostly because of injury, just occasionally because of form. To describe him as a marginal cricketer would be ridiculous, but he has, at times, been a marginal presence.

If the 2009 Ashes series has become Flintoff's Ashes then it is not because, like Botham's Ashes of '81, of performance but because of a decision to announce his retirement before the Lord's Test ensured that would be so: demanding the spotlight without the deeds to back it up. There have been a lot of column inches about a player who has scored one half-century and taken 7 wickets at 48.57. Flintoff is an industry now, with his own PR machine, as much as a cricketer.

Perhaps this series is more of a reflection of his career as a whole than those who would shower him with greatness would care to admit. A drink-related incident to begin with, the circus surrounding his retirement, the great spell at Lord's, injured since but still hogging the headlines. During this summer, he has touched greatness and been occasionally inspirational; it has been so throughout his career.

It is no disgrace to fall short when measured against the very best that the game has to offer. But to be the very best you have to give more than he has been prepared to give. He never really set out to achieve greatness, doesn't yearn for it in the same way as Kevin Pietersen. Flintoff plays for enjoyment, the company of mates, the baubles that success brings and for days like today, when the deciding Test in an Ashes series is there to be won.

Long after England's players had practised, showered, interviewed and departed, Andrew Strauss could be found in the nets, fine-tuning a technique he is certain will hold up under pressure over the next five days. It can be a lonely job, this captaincy lark, although Strauss had Andy Flower for company, the team director running in hard, shouting 'Hilfenhaus', 'Siddle' or 'Clark', and throwing balls rapidly from a dozen yards or so. Strauss must feel as if he has been a target all summer.

They left the field together after a prolonged session and it was fitting to see them wandering off in close conversation, for they have developed an incredibly tight relationship since they were thrust together after the turmoil of the Kevin Pietersen–Peter Moores era. It is to their great credit that, eight months on, their England team stand five winning days of cricket away from regaining the Ashes.

Neither are renowned history students, but if they were they would take both comfort and pain from the past. In the past hundred years, there have been only eight occasions when both teams have been level going into the final Test of an Ashes series. Five of those occasions have been at The Oval, where England have won three matches to Australia's two, regaining the Ashes in 1926 and 1953.

Much has happened in their short stewardship that could

have de-railed their project – 51 all out in Jamaica, the circus surrounding Andrew Flintoff's injuries and retirement, the issues thrown up by the Indian Premier League and the injury to Kevin Pietersen. But both have maintained what Hemingway called grace under pressure, showing a calmness and unflappability that will hold them in good stead throughout a match that is sure to be emotionally draining.

Headingley was a low point to match Sabina Park, but still Strauss and Flower refused to panic. 'Home team, service and repair' was emblazoned on the sponsors' sightscreen the day before this Test, but the only servicing post-Headingley has been to Flintoff's knee and the only repair job has been to the number three position, where Ian Bell will replace Ravi Bopara, allowing Jonathan Trott to make his debut at number five, Paul Collingwood sandwiching between them.

Similar faces there may be, but Strauss has an awkward decision or two to make before the toss – not so much Sherlock Holmes's two-pipe problem, but a two-spinner predicament. The pitch is grassless, dry and the colour of a Rich Tea biscuit. It looks, to all intents and purposes, like a two-spinner pitch (that is to say, a batting pitch upon which the captain would like to have a balanced attack), but do England trust Monty Panesar in his current form?

It is a measure of Panesar's recent decline that such conditions give rise to head-scratching. Before the series, spin was supposedly Australia's Achilles' heel and England's point of strength, but a meagre return of one for 246 in 73 unproductive overs of spin between Graeme Swann and Panesar at Cardiff, and the better-than-expected form of Nathan Hauritz, led to that plan being quickly shelved.

Hauritz is unlikely to play at The Oval, as Marcus North offers a decent alternative, and Australia will be loath to change a winning side, but, for England, Panesar's return would create problems. Who would miss out? To judge from the look on Graham Onions's face yesterday, he has already been given the bad news, and Strauss talked up Stephen Harmison's chances at a ground that has been good to him. Stuart Broad would be the fall guy in that instance, but he was one of the few success stories at Headingley where he took six wickets and scored a half-century. And if Panesar does play, Flintoff becomes the third seamer, with all the extra overs such a move entails.

Strauss insisted that Flintoff is fit to play a full part in proceedings and it was the all-rounder, inevitably, on whom most questions centred. Asked whether the sentiment of the occasion presented a problem, Strauss agreed, saying that his team had to guard against emotion taking over, that they play best when playing 'emotionless' cricket, when the head rules the heart.

But, surely, this is wrong. Home advantage, the notoriously patriotic Oval crowd and Flintoff's impending retirement are England's overwhelming – some might say, only – advantages. Strauss should encourage his team to ride an emotional wave over the next five days, much as Kevin Pietersen did here during his innings of 158 four years ago, hoping that the fervent support lifts his players' game beyond the humdrum.

No player in recent memory has communicated with the crowd better than Flintoff, nobody plays his cricket more emotionally, and he warmed up for his final fling in Tests by bowling sharply in the nets. He knows that his reputation is already made, but that the next five days could add some extra gloss –

and a few noughts to the cost of his personal appearances – and he looks hungry to do well.

The stakes are as high for Ricky Ponting as they are for Strauss and Flintoff. Should Australia be beaten, Ponting would become only the second Australia captain to lose the Ashes twice on English soil – hardly the kind of postscript such a fine cricketer would like to see on his CV. This may not be his last Test on English soil, as Australia are due to play Pakistan here next year, but it may well be his last Ashes Test and he said that he could not remember being more excited for a match.

If it ends in victory, or at least with the Ashes in safe keeping, it would be a triumph to rank alongside any he has achieved as captain, especially given the dampened expectations at the start of the tour and his personnel, who are not so much sprinkled with stardust as dandruff. After going behind at Lord's, Ponting and his team have held their nerve, worked hard so that many of their big-game players are peaking at the right time, and now he has the opportunity to banish the memory of 2005.

The heart says England, but the head – the emotionless head that Strauss wants his team to play with – says Australia.

Day 1, Thursday 20 August

Close of play: England 307 for 8

You cannot win a Test on Day One, Andrew Strauss said before the match, failing to add the coda that you can certainly lose one. To judge from the nervy atmosphere that pervaded The

Oval throughout the day, the crowd watching in a kind of silent, fraught, nail-biting way from first ball to last that was in stark contrast to the wild triumphalism of 2005, it was a fear that was never far away.

It is England's batting line-up minus Kevin Pietersen that is the cause of the nervousness, and it was England's batting line-up minus Pietersen that was under the spotlight. Once again they were found wanting, half-centuries from Strauss and Ian Bell, and a perky 41 from Jonathan Trott on debut, not enough to mask the feeling that an opportunity had been missed. Just one hundred throughout the series is a damning statistic, one upon which not many series wins have been fashioned.

Strangely, though, England's chances of regaining the Ashes were actually better last evening than if they had finished, say, just three down on a traditional Oval belter. Already the ball is turning significantly and occasionally biting into the surface and disturbing the top, reminiscent of the 1997 pitch upon which Australia could not score 124 in the last innings for victory. Because of that, it is not easy to say what a good first-innings score actually is, although it is probably something nearer 400 than 300. What is certain is that batting cannot get any easier. Weather permitting, this will not be a draw and Australia's first innings holds the key to the match.

Nor was there a fairytale contribution from Andrew Flintoff, although the silence that greeted his exit, in contrast to the resounding ovation that accompanied him to the middle, was the surest sign that England supporters expect their hero to have a second innings before this game is done. Flintoff was desperate to adorn this day with some extravagant stroke play, but he was rendered strokeless by Mitchell Johnson's determination to pin him to the crease with some fast, short-pitched bowling and he flayed, flat-footed and woodenly, at his nineteenth delivery, and departed for just seven.

Given that Strauss's fourth correct call in five games conferred a significant advantage, Australia will be pleased with their day's work. England lunched ominously at 108 for one, but the last two sessions belonged to the visitors, seven wickets falling through a combination of disciplined line bowling and sharp fielding, four of them to Peter Siddle, who put in his best performance of the summer. Only the over-rate and the frequent overstepping of the front line would have creased Ricky Ponting's brow.

If one moment summed up Australia's day, it was the dismissal of Trott, who was brilliantly run out by Simon Katich at short leg. Trott had played as well as could be expected once his early nerves had disappeared, and he was eyeing a half-century when he turned Marcus North into the leg side and set off for a run. Katich dived, pounced and in a blur transferred the ball to his left hand and threw down the stumps. It was an opportunistic moment on a day when Australia took the chances that came their way.

After the horrors of Headingley, England desperately needed a bright start and it was a more serendipitous morning all round for the England captain. There were no last-minute injuries to upset his rhythm or a delayed toss to scramble his brain, and it was no surprise to see him settle down to his task, clipping through the leg side when Siddle strayed in line and driving fluently down the ground.

The only blot on his morning was the departure of his opening partner, Alastair Cook, who once again found the Australians' probing outside off stump too hot to handle, Siddle finding his edge with a ball that slanted across the left-hander. Cook has not had a series to remember and is at present banging his head against the glass ceiling of his technical deficiencies.

Strauss's temperament has never been in question – remember his first-innings hundred in this corresponding fixture four years ago – and he rattled off ten boundaries in the morning in an 89-ball half-century. So well was he playing, and such is his proven ability to convert fifties to hundreds, that it was a surprise to see him offering his bat to Ben Hilfenhaus shortly after lunch and feathering a catch to Brad Haddin. Replays showed Hilfenhaus to have overstepped the crease comfortably, but that does not excuse the limpness of the stroke.

Strauss's dismissal brought Paul Collingwood and Bell together, players in need of a score to quell the doubts that they lack the presence or punch to succeed in Pietersen's absence. Bell had other worries, no doubt, the words Ashes, Australia and The Oval bringing to mind the pair he scored here four years ago. It is the kind of memory that is burnished on the brain, and he began scratchily as if the years between those fixtures had not taken place.

Standing taller to counter Johnson's inswing, he found it difficult to duck under the liberal sprinkling of bouncers that came his way, and was perilously close to gloving a leg-side catch before he had scored. It was good to see him struggling and surviving, though, and fluency came eventually, as it usually does. With Collingwood into double figures, Ponting settled for containment, sure in the knowledge that England had to make the running.

It was a waiting game that served Australia's captain well and highlighted exactly why England miss Pietersen's boldness, unorthodoxy and ability to take the game to the opposition. With Australia's seam bowlers holding a firm line outside off stump, to packed off-side fields, the scoring rate stalled so that frustration crept in and wickets followed. Siddle enticed Collingwood to skew a drive to gully and then found Bell's inside edge, the ball cannoning into his stumps. Matt Prior played early and one-handed at a Johnson slower ball and Graeme Swann edged the final delivery on the day into Haddin's gloves.

Eight down was three wickets too many, the grimness of the news tempered by the thought that this is the result pitch England have been praying for.

Day 2, Friday 21 August

Close of play: England 332 and 58 for 3; Australia 160

At precisely 3.15 pm, on a glorious late summer's afternoon, The Oval crammed to bursting and the Ashes on the line, a bugler sounded out a solitary tune and the crowd burst into a spontaneous rendition of the National Anthem. For the first time in this final match of the series, the mood had turned from nervous fretting to one of supreme confidence, and for the first time since the opening session of the fourth Test at Headingley, the consensus was, and is, that England will regain the Ashes.

This is a series that has had more twists and turns, plots and subplots, than a Len Deighton thriller, but when Australia lost ten wickets for 87 in 20 overs in the afternoon, granting England a first-innings lead of 172, it felt like the storyline had taken its final, decisive turn. There was still half the match and three days' cricket to be played, but England had manoeuvred themselves, though a combination of skill, luck and Australian fragility, into what, surely, was an unbeatable position.

But England do not like to give their supporters too easy a ride. With Australia on their knees, and the atmosphere triumphant, England conspired to introduce some nervousness again, losing three early wickets in their second innings: Alastair Cook completed his poor series, playing across a turner from Marcus North, edging to slip and confirming Australia's error in leaving out their specialist spinner, and Ian Bell and Paul Collingwood gave Simon Katich two catches at short leg off Mitchell Johnson. Australia will not go down without a fight.

Bell was unlucky after turning the ball neatly off his hips, Collingwood not so, after getting in an almighty, undignified tangle to a short ball that confirmed his exposure at number four. Only Andrew Strauss appeared unaffected by the conditions, which are deteriorating by the over, or the situation, which remained fraught. He was unbeaten on 32, England's lead at the close 230. It is a position from which a win should be a formality.

Maybe the stage is set for an Andrew Flintoff cameo to consolidate the gains made during an astonishing afternoon when Australia suffered a very English-style collapse. This was supposed to be Flintoff's match, but nobody, clearly, had told Stuart

Broad, who bowled throughout the afternoon session, taking five for 37 in 12 overs of superb swing and cut that destroyed the cream of Australian batsmanship, confirmed his position as the heir to Fred's throne and his place in Ashes folklore. Maybe the torch was being passed before our very eyes: Flintoff to Broad, all-rounder to all-rounder. It was a time, instead, for youth over experience, promise over the past.

There was little in the morning session to suggest that such a collapse was in the offing. England had added 25 to their overnight total, giving them a final return that seemed, like Chesterton's umbrella (an unmanageable walking stick when shut and an inadequate tent when open), neither one thing nor t'other – neither gargantuan enough to rubber-stamp success, nor flimsy enough to dampen all hope.

Australia, then, got through the remainder of the session unscathed. Sure, the occasional ball had dusted the top and Shane Watson had given off an early air of impermanence before settling to his task with that doughty fighter, Katich, for company. Flintoff, relegating Stephen Harmison to first change and bowling urgently with the new ball, might have had Watson leg-before twice but for umpiring intransigence, but Australia went to lunch, three minutes early because of some light rain, 61 without loss.

After a break of 55 minutes while the showers cleared and the groundstaff dried the outfield, Strauss decided to replace Graeme Swann with Broad and that was the catalyst for the procession that followed: Watson was trapped on the crease in Broad's first over; in his third, Ricky Ponting dragged on from wide; the very next over, Mike Hussey was palpably leg-before, playing with pad and not bat to a ball nipping back; then, in Broad's next over, Michael Clarke played too soon into the hands of Jonathan Trott at short extra cover, and in his ninth over, Brad Haddin played all around a full, swinging ball, the death rattle confirming his worst fears.

At the other end, Graeme Swann fed, as baby to a mother's breast, off Broad's inspiration, and the most perfect spin bowling conditions imaginable, taking three wickets of his own in that session, all of them left-handers. Marcus North, pushing forward, was unlucky that umpire Asad Rauf failed to see a clear inside edge, and it was another inside edge, ballooning up off the pad, that brought Katich's resistance to a close, Cook taking the offering at short leg. Mitchell Johnson pushed forward and edged to Matt Prior and 61 without loss had become 133 for eight. In those 24 overs the destination of the urn was, surely, settled.

Such events call for an explanation. The surface of the pitch, never stable on the first day, had become even more crumbly on the second, and although not many deliveries misbehaved badly, doubts had clearly crept into Australian minds. Watson's constant prodding at the pitch early on betrayed their fears. In such conditions, it is harder to get in than to stay in, so a cluster of wickets is always a possibility and, as we have seen in this series during the first innings at Lord's and at Edgbaston, this Australia are more fragile than their predecessors.

Strauss found the perfect combination in Broad, whose manipulation of the seam and ability to bowl cutters was perfectly suited to the receptive conditions, and Swann, who revelled in the pressure and the expectation. The captain enjoyed the chance to squeeze, too, testing Michael Clarke's impatience with a shrewdly set field, Clarke's exquisite form ill-suited to the conditions that demanded more fight than fluency.

Lady luck was with England, too, Stuart Clark, the ninth wicket, joining North in the hard-done-to camp when he was given out caught at short leg even though there was clear daylight between bat and ball. By the day's end, there was clear daylight between the teams.

Day 3, Saturday 22 August

Close of play: England 332 and 373 for 9 dec; Australia 160 and 80 for 0

Sport is usually swift and emphatic in its resolutions: a little under 20 seconds, for instance, is all you need to realise that Usain Bolt is the quickest man on the planet over 200 metres. The Ashes, though, demand a longer concentration span, and after 21 days of cricket, the pendulum swinging this way and that, the final equation is upon us: Australia must make more runs than any team has ever made in the fourth innings of a match in the history of first-class cricket, or bat out two days for a draw, otherwise they will relinquish their hold on the Ashes.

Andrew Strauss called a halt to England's second innings late in the third session of play, at the moment that Jonathan Trott's debut hundred was brought to a close, and he did so with England's lead a mammoth 545. No doubt he was hoping for a couple of wickets in the 20 overs that remained, but Australia's openers fought through to the close undefeated, Australia's score a healthy-looking 80 without loss.

Simon Katich and Shane Watson, this makeshift opening pair, had set out from their changing room in the manner of men who would be gone for some time, and in seeing their team to the close they deserve the greatest credit. Nor did they suffer any undue alarms, only the odd ball spitting, as if fat from a frying pan, and the occasional edge falling short of a fielder. Mostly, they were untroubled, something that will give Ricky Ponting great heart as he attempts to avoid the fate of Billy Murdoch, the only Australian captain to lose two Ashes series in England.

As well as Australia played in the late-afternoon sunshine, England hold all the aces. The pitch has slowed a little and although groundsman Bill Gordon's wasteland has not produced anything really brutish or nasty, it is still a difficult surface on which to bat, especially as the ball gets older. Spin will hold the key, and patience will be important. The wickets will probably come slowly, but they will surely come. Pessimists will point to a third day that garnered 395 runs for just nine wickets, but batting fourth under pressure is a totally different ball game to batting third when your noses are comfortably in front.

England began the day well in the ascendancy, of course, and that they ended it in such a commanding position was largely down to Trott, who confounded those who would not have had a debutant playing in such a critical fixture, by playing in the manner of a toddler on a family outing. He walked out to bat with the unflappable Strauss at the start of the day, and remained until the end of England's innings, when he cut Stuart Clark to

Marcus North in the gully with 119 runs to his name, becoming only the 18th England player to score a hundred on his Test debut, the first against Australia since Graham Thorpe at Trent Bridge, 16 years ago.

He played so well that we must doff our hats to the selectors, first and foremost. They ignored the calls for experience – pah! who needs experience – and stuck to their guns. They had seen something in Trott and he repaid their faith. Spin, said some, is his Achilles' heel, but he played North, who finished with four wickets to further embarrass the Australian selectors, better than most, and mainly off the back foot, which was wise given the amount of turn and the number of predatory catchers close to home.

When the first ball of the day to Trott from Peter Siddle exploded off a length before landing in the Brad Haddin's gloves after a huge appeal, it seemed that not just Trott's but England's innings would be short-lived. In fact, the ball had clipped his trouser leg – a superb piece of umpiring, this – rather than the edge of the bat as all eleven Australians were convinced it had done. After that, the odds on a wicketless first session would have been generous indeed, but England were minutes from just that when Strauss drove North into the hands of Michael Clarke at slip. Strauss swished his bat in frustration but, with two fifties, he has had a good match and done his bit.

Once Matt Prior had run himself out, the stage was set for Andrew Flintoff, who ran down The Oval steps and out into the sunshine to an enormous ovation, the kind which confirmed, if any confirmation was necessary, the place he occupies in English supporters' hearts. Ricky Ponting, touchingly, shook the hero's hand at the crease, confirmation, too, that the Australians have admired the cut of his jib. Coming in with a lead of 372, Flintoff could throw the blade with merry abandon and he left the crowd with a few meaty-sized memories. It was in attempting one more over mid-on that he holed out, and he wandered off to another gargantuan reception. He'll have earache tonight.

Stuart Broad, fittingly, replaced him, and he and Graeme Swann then enjoyed themselves in the sun, Swann especially causing Australia much irritation with a 55-ball 63 that included some hefty blows through and over the off side. It will have done his confidence no harm at all ahead of a day in which he must make his primary skill count.

With Broad hoisting North to Ponting, and Swann late on a Ben Hilfenhaus bouncer, there was a momentary fear that Trott would run out of partners. He had battled throughout the afternoon, taking his score from 50 to 83, and he was still ten shy of his hundred when Jimmy Anderson walked in to bat. But now Trott took control, although he nearly played on to leg stump on 97, the ball dribbling off inside edge, pad and just past his wicket. A leg-side clip brought him his moment and it was celebrated with just the right amount of vigour and decorum, after which he spanked Stuart Clark down the ground for a brace of fours, the best of the day.

It was a day he and his family will remember for ever. The cameras panned to his mother, who was in tears, his wife who was in WAGdom and the crowd who had welcomed him whole-heartedly into the England fold.

Trott's pleasure was equalled only by Ponting's pain. The Australian captain had taken a nasty blow to the face when field-ing at silly point and was now sporting a pair of bruised and swollen lips, something the crowd, with its usual lack of grace, found amusing. Does the Australian captain have one more innings in him? Can he inspire his team to a miracle run-chase? The odds are stacked against him. More pain to follow.

Day 4, Sunday 23 August

Close of play: England 332 and 373 for 9 dec; Australia 160 and 348

Lord's is the home of English cricket, and the sanctuary for the most prized possession in the sport; but it is The Oval where the most memorable Ashes moments have come. At 11 minutes to six, on a glorious late summer's evening, with just a hint of triumphalism in the air, the England cricket team, 2009 vintage, gave us another.

Mike Hussey, the epitome of the Aussie battler, a man who had come to the crease on a pair and with his career under threat, was unbeaten with a hundred to his name. He had just the last man, Ben Hilfenhaus, for company and his team were still 197 runs adrift. Hussey pushed forward to Graeme Swann, found glove and inside edge instead of the middle of the blade; the ball popped up to Alastair Cook at short leg; the catch was taken and 22 days of cricket had delivered their final, irreversible judgment.

Followers of English cricket will be able to reel off iconic images down the years at this famous old ground: colourful ones of, say, Michael Vaughan and David Gower, and a monochrome one, perhaps, of Len Hutton holding aloft the urn.

Now they will be able to add another name to that list – that of Andrew Strauss, who, 15 minutes after the victory moment, stood in front of the old pavilion, as Vaughan had done four years before, holding a replica of sport's tiniest trophy high above his head.

It was a victory for the England team, but above all it was a victory for Strauss. He went away from the podium laden with baubles, not just the urn, but the man of the series award for his calm leadership and his 474 runs at the top of the order at 52.66, and the Compton-Miller Award, previous recipients of which have been Andrew Flintoff and Ricky Ponting, given to the man on either side who made the most impact upon the series.

Strauss had taken on the England captaincy after a period of turmoil under Kevin Pietersen and Peter Moores and, now, only eight months later, was enjoying what he will surely look back upon as his proudest moment as a cricketer: winning the Ashes as a player one thing; winning them as captain quite another. The Ashes is the biggest test of an England cricketer, captaining in the Ashes the biggest test of character and temperament of them all. And what a job he has done.

While Strauss and the England team set off on the lap of honour, which will replace the open-top bus parade and Trafalgar Square as a suitably sober celebration for these straitened times, Ponting made his lonely walk up the pavilion steps. He has become only the second Australian captain after Billy Murdoch to lose the Ashes twice in England and, no doubt, there will be questions asked about his leadership now. But, on the field and off it, he has been immense this summer. There has to be a loser, but Ponting's countrymen should be proud of their captain's efforts.

Ponting batted yesterday like a man who believed in the impossible. He had come to the crease after the early loss of Simon Katich and Shane Watson, both leg-before, the first to Swann the second to Stuart Broad, who was later named man of the match for his five wickets in Australia's first innings. There was something deeply heroic about the way Australia's captain set about his task, his lips bruised and bloodied from the blow he had taken the day before at short leg; the situation hopeless really, not that you would have known it from the way he continued to come at England's bowlers.

Ponting was playing for his reputation, of course, and he might have felt there was a debt to repay, depending on how influential a voice his had been in selection. He walked out to a standing ovation that was not far short in its feeling from the one Flintoff had accepted a day earlier, proper recognition of his services and his position as a great of the game. He gave a performance to match, too, in conditions that were as far removed from the pitches of his youth as it was possible to be.

Ponting might have had to adjust his technique according to the circumstances, but he was not prepared to yield any of the aggressive intent that is programmed into him and his fifty came from just 76 balls, a remarkable rate given the conditions and Australia's position. If captaincy is about inspiring through personal performance, which it is to some extent, then no captain could have done more for his team yesterday and the manner of his dismissal, run out when called for a quick single by Hussey, would have been heartbreaking for the dressing room.

Ponting's run-out at Trent Bridge in 2005 was widely assumed to be the moment that England realised they could win the Ashes; now his run-out by Andrew Flintoff, moving around from mid-on like a 20-year-old rather than a man in his last Test, was the moment that the destiny of the Ashes was decided. It was Hussey's call as he clipped to mid-on, but Ponting was guilty, momentarily, of ball watching and that moment's hesitation cost him his wicket. As the third umpire delivered his verdict, there was just the merest hint of reproach in a glance towards Hussey, then Ponting left the field, as he came, to a standing ovation.

Hussey continued his remarkable defiance, but the lifeblood had drained out of Australia now. Michael Clarke followed soon after his captain, run out as he danced down the pitch to Swann, his clip to mid-wicket cannoning off Cook at short leg, whereupon Strauss at leg slip pounced and threw down the stumps. Marcus North was stumped smartly by Matt Prior as he swept with his back foot on the line and Brad Haddin clipped airily to deep mid-wicket. This pitch was no place for a tail-ender to thrive, and the end came quickly then, Stephen Harmison mopping up the crumbs before Swann's dismissal of Hussey.

This, then, was the fairytale ending that Flintoff craved, and his was a scene-stealing effort of which a late-version Marlon Brando would have been proud. Moving and swooping like a primed athlete for possibly the last time, he threw down Ponting's stumps and stood, as he had at Lord's, with his arms aloft while he waited for his colleagues to embrace him. There were no runs and wickets for him yesterday, but the gods had granted him, out of recognition for a remarkable career, the day's defining image.

The Aftermath

It looked the same, but felt different. Same ground, same podium and some of the same people but, four years on, there was quite a different feeling to the celebrations of 2009. There was, said a colleague in the press box, a lot of joy but an absence of ecstasy. It was a good way of putting it and it felt better somehow.

Maybe it was something to do with the times in which we live. Four years ago we were living in the middle of a debt-fuelled orgy of consumerism, the kind of age in which an open-topped bus parade and drink-fuelled party at Trafalgar Square were fitting conclusions to a wonderfully topsy-turvy series. Now we are a little wiser, a little more sober. Credit-crunched, a lap of honour will have to do.

Some of it is down to the destination of the urn itself. In 2005, England had not won the Ashes for 18 years, and the competition, because of its uncompetitive nature had almost become an irrelevance in world cricketing terms. Now we are in the middle of a period of pass the parcel, the trophy having changed hands on the last three occasions for only the second time in its history. There have always been periods of dominance, mostly Australian, but it is a contest again. Normal service has been resumed. Celebrations need not go overboard; there is a degree of expectation now.

Some of the players are certainly a little older and a little wiser. Four years ago, Kevin Pietersen was at the forefront of celebrations, his hair long and with a bright blue skunk line down the middle. On Sunday, he was at The Oval, but his foot was in plastercast and his celebrations were muted because of it. He had played but not really performed or contributed. With an Achilles' heel, literally, where he didn't have one before, he is aware of his own sporting mortality now.

Freddie Flintoff is older, too, and, we trust, a little wiser. To look at his features, he didn't look much different to four years before, a great ginger beard shielding his face from the sun, but on the field it was clear that an ageing cricketer was playing out his Test career for the last time. Apart from when he swooped and threw down Ricky Ponting's stumps, he looked, suddenly, very old, limping around the outer and unable to summon up the will with the ball. Four years is a long time in sport.

In the four years between these two great Oval moments, England have not really travelled very far at all. And that is now the question for Andrew Strauss and Andy Flower, the men who take most credit for this summer's achievement: is winning the Ashes the end of something, as it was in 2005, or the beginning?

It will be very interesting to see, noted the late Bob Woolmer as he prepared his Pakistan team for England's first post-2005 Ashes series, how they cope with success. Woolmer, as a former England player who had coached South Africa, that most driven of sporting nations, knew a little of the English sporting psyche, and he had his England team spot on. They didn't cope with it very well.

Partly this was down to injuries – cruelly, to Simon Jones,

and to Marcus Trescothick, Michael Vaughan and others – but the germ of England's faltering progress after 2005 could be found in that orgy of self-congratulation, in the MBEs handed out like confetti at a wedding party, and the commercialisation that followed. England's players had not known success like it and they didn't know how to cope.

As the man who has been at the heart of both contests, Strauss knows what it is like to win. He knows, too, a little of what it is like to win and then lose focus and it is his job now to ensure that does not happen again. A starting point is an acceptance that England are not a top-notch cricket team. 'We are playing the number one ranked team,' intoned Flower throughout the series. But Australia have plummeted to fourth now, a more accurate reflection of where their talents lie. England beat a mid-ranking team, as well they ought on home soil.

So, Strauss's team is a work in progress. They have heart and spirit in abundance and an excellent leadership team, both good starting points. The batting, though, is a problem. Alastair Cook has hit a glass ceiling and looks no more competent outside off stump than he did two years ago. There was just one knock of significance from him in the series. He has stalled. Paul Collingwood, to whom it must be remembered the debt of Cardiff is owed, was exposed at number four, just as his leaden-footed, bottom-handed technique was exposed after that match. Ravi Bopara, in whom so much faith has been stowed, has had to be withdrawn from the firing line twice in the space of two years. Pietersen may come back to full fitness; he may not.

England need to work out how to balance their team post-Flintoff. Is Stuart Broad good enough to bat at number seven?

More pertinently, is he good enough to bat at number seven, given the personnel at numbers one to six? And can he avoid the celebrity trap now that Lily Allen and others have noticed his good looks? And what of Stephen Harmison, who nipped in with some late wickets at The Oval. Central contract or not? And who will be England's second spinner, if Monty Panesar cannot be trusted with his place on the mother of all 'bunsen burners'?

This sounds like rather a lot of questions for a team that have just won the Ashes. But, there is no better time to tinker than when you are winning. As Australia demonstrated so ably after Headingley, 'don't change a winning team' is just about the dumbest aphorism in sport. A touch of selectorial ruthlessness – no Collingwood to South Africa, perhaps? – would send the clearest possible message that this Ashes triumph is the start of something special rather than the end.

SCORECARD

ENGLAND v AUSTRALIA

At The Oval, London, on 20, 21, 22, 23 August.

Result: **ENGLAND won by 197 runs.** Toss: England.

ENGLAND	First Innings	Runs	Mins	Balls	4/6
*A.J.Strauss	c Haddin b Hilfenhaus	55	128	101	11
A.N.Cook	c Ponting b Siddle	10	19	12	2
I.R.Bell	b Siddle	72	222	137	10
P.D.Collingwood	c Hussey b Siddle	24	89	65	3
I.J.L.Trott	run out	41	125	81	5
†M.J.Prior	c Watson b Johnson	18	57	33	2
A.Flintoff	c Haddin b Johnson	7	21	19	1
S.C.J.Broad	c Ponting b Hilfenhaus	37	89	69	5
G.P.Swann	c Haddin b Siddle	18	43	28	2
J.M.Anderson	lbw b Hilfenhaus	0	5	6	–
S.J.Harmison	not out	12	17	12	3
Extras (B 12, LB 5, W 3, NB 18)		38			
Total (90.5 overs; 414 mins)		**332**			

Fall of Wickets: 12-1 (Cook, 5.3 overs); 114-2 (Strauss, 28.1 overs); 176-3 (Collingwood, 47.5 overs); 181-4 (Bell, 53.5 overs); 229-5 (Prior, 65.3 overs); 247-6 (Flintoff, 69.4,overs); 268-7 (Trott, 74.2 overs); 307-8 (Swann, 85.3 overs); 308-9 (Anderson, 86.6 overs); 332-10 (Broad, 90.5 overs).

AUSTRALIA	Overs	Mdns	Runs	Wkts	Econ	Strike
Hilfenhaus	21.5	5	71	3	3.25	43.7
Siddle	21	6	75	4	3.57	31.5
Clark	14	5	41	0	2.93	–
Johnson	15	0	69	2	4.60	45.0
North	14	3	33	0	2.36	–
Watson	5	0	26	0	5.20	–

AUSTRALIA	First Innings	Runs	Mins	Balls	4/6
S.R.Watson	lbw b Broad	34	94	69	7
S.M.Katich	c Cook b Swann	50	169	107	7
*R.T.Ponting	b Broad	8	20	15	1
M.E.K.Hussey	lbw b Broad	0	6	3	–
M.J.Clarke	c Trott b Broad	3	9	7	–
M.J.North	lbw b Swann	8	28	17	1
†B.J.Haddin	b Broad	1	13	9	–
M.G.Johnson	c Prior b Swann	11	27	24	2
P.M.Siddle	not out	26	54	38	5
S.R.Clark	c Cook b Swann	6	14	8	1
B.W.Hilfenhaus	b Flintoff	6	10	21	1
Extras (B 1, LB 5, NB 1)		7			
Total (52.5 overs; 226 mins)		**160**			

Fall of Wickets: 73-1 (Watson, 22.6 overs); 85-2 (Ponting, 26.6 overs); 89-3 (Hussey, 28.3 overs); 93-4 (Clarke, 30.2 overs); 108-5 (North, 35.3 overs); 109-6 (Katich, 37.1 overs); 111-7 (Haddin, 38.4 overs); 131-8 (Johnson, 43.5 overs); 143-9 (Clark, 47.3 overs); 160-10 (Hilfenhaus, 52.5 overs).

ENGLAND	Overs	Mdns	Runs	Wkts	Econ	Strike
Anderson	9	3	29	0	3.22	–
Flintoff	13.5	4	35	1	2.53	83.0
Swann	14	3	38	4	2.71	21.0
Harmison	4	1	15	0	3.75	–
Broad	12	1	37	5	3.08	14.4

Fifth Test, The Oval 20–23 August

ENGLAND	Second Innings	Runs	Mins	Balls	4/6
*A.J.Strauss	c Clarke b North	75	226	191	8
A.N.Cook	c Clarke b North	9	49	35	–
I.R.Bell	c Katich b Johnson	4	13	7	1
P.D.Collingwood	c Katich b Johnson	1	9	7	–
I.J.L.Trott	c North b Clark	119	331	193	12
†M.J.Prior	run out	4	16	9	1
A.Flintoff	c Siddle b North	22	24	18	4
S.C.J.Broad	c Ponting b North	29	43	35	5
G.P.Swann	c Haddin b Hilfenhaus	63	57	55	9
J.M.Anderson	not out	15	34	29	2
S.J.Harmison					
Extras (B 1, LB 15, W 7, NB 9)		32			
Total (9 wkts dec; 95 overs; 408 mins)		**373**			

Fall of Wickets: 27-1 (Cook, 12.3 overs); 34-2 (Bell, 15.4 overs); 39-3 (Collingwood, 17.3 overs); 157-4 (Strauss, 54.3 overs); 168-5 (Prior, 57.6 overs); 200-6 (Flintoff, 64.1 overs); 243-7 (Broad, 74.2 overs); 333-8 (Swann, 87.4 overs); 373-9 (Trott, 94.6 overs).

AUSTRALIA	Overs	Mdns	Runs	Wkts	Econ	Strike
Hilfenhaus	11	1	58	1	5.27	66.0
Siddle	17	3	69	0	4.06	–
North	30	4	98	4	3.27	45.0
Johnson	17	1	60	2	3.53	51.0
Katich	5	2	9	0	1.80	–
Clark	12	2	43	1	3.58	72.0
Clarke	3	0	20	0	6.67	–

AUSTRALIA	Second Innings	Runs	Mins	Balls	4/6
S.R.Watson	lbw b Broad	40	101	81	6
S.M.Katich	lbw b Swann	43	98	68	7
*R.T.Ponting	run out	66	157	103	10
M.E.K.Hussey	c Cook b Swann	121	328	263	14
M.J.Clarke	run out	0	5	4	–
M.J.North	st Prior b Swann	10	31	24	2
†B.J.Haddin	c Strauss b Swann	34	95	49	6
M.G.Johnson	c Collingwood b Harmison	0	5	5	–
P.M.Siddle	c Flintoff b Harmison	10	14	14	1
S.R.Clark	c Cook b Harmison	0	1	1	–
B.W.Hilfenhaus	not out	4	10	8	1
Extras (B 7, LB 7, NB 6)		20			
Total (102.2 overs; 431 mins)		**348**			

Fall of Wickets: 86-1 (Katich, 23.6 overs); 90-2 (Watson, 24.3 overs); 217-3 (Ponting, 63.6 overs); 220-4 (Clarke, 64.5 overs); 236-5 (North, 72.2 overs); 327-6 (Haddin, 94.4 overs); 327-7 (Johnson, 95.5 overs); 343-8 (Siddle, 99.4 overs); 343-9 (Clark, 99.5 overs); 348-10 (Hussey, 102.2 overs).

ENGLAND	Overs	Mdns	Runs	Wkts	Econ	Strike
Anderson	12	2	46	0	3.83	–
Flintoff	11	1	42	0	3.82	–
Harmison	16	5	54	3	3.37	32.0
Swann	40.2	8	120	4	2.98	60.5
Broad	22	4	71	1	3.23	132.0
Collingwood	1	0	1	0	1.00	–

Umpires: Asad Rauf (*Pakistan*) (26) and B.F.Bowden (*New Zealand*) (56). Referee: R.S.Madugalle (*Sri Lanka*) (111). Man of the Match: S.C.J.Broad.

The Oval Test Facts:

- Australia's first innings total of 160 was their lowest Ashes total since they were bowled out for 104 at The Oval in 1997.

- Stuart Broad's five for 37 was his second successive five-for and his third in all Test matches.

- Jonathan Trott became the 18th England player to score a century on his Test debut, and the first since Graham Thorpe against Australia in 1993.

- James Anderson's record of 54 innings at the start of his career without being dismissed for nought came to an end in the first innings.

- Mike Hussey scored his first Test century after 28 innings without one; it was his second Ashes hundred and his tenth overall.

- The Oval is England's most successful Ashes venue, with 16 wins and just six defeats in 35 Tests.

- Ricky Ponting became the first Australia captain to lose the Ashes twice since Billy Murdoch in the 1890s.

Conclusion

The morning after the day before, The Oval was deserted save the groundstaff watering the pitch and removing the debris from the outfield, the television companies filling time on a scheduled day of cricket, and the dressing-room attendants waiting for England's cricketers to return to remove their belongings.

By ten o'clock in the morning nobody had returned, since, although the celebrations were more muted than four years before (Andrew Flintoff, for example, looked positively chipper at his early morning press conference), the England players were enjoying a well deserved lie-in. At noon, Andrew Strauss appeared and said he was 'absolutely knackered'. He looked it.

The respective changing rooms spoke of victory and defeat. Australia's had already been emptied, save a few old shirts and, with the one-day series looming, white pads that were now redundant. It was as if they could not wait to leave a ground that has not treated them well in recent years. The Oval has brought Australia defeats in 1993 and 1997 (both dead rubbers), a draw in 2005 that gave England the Ashes, and now a defeat in 2009 in a rubber that was very much alive. Australia's dressing room was bare and cold and devoid of life.

In contrast, England's dressing room resembled that of a team who had dallied long into the evening, sharing stories, swapping tales and generally revelling in that feeling of supreme team spirit that comes in the aftermath of victory. Kit was strewn everywhere, only Jonathan Trott's bags were neatly arranged. There were mementos to pick up, four pieces of memorabilia gifted by the MCC, one to Andrew Flintoff on his five wickets at Lord's, one to Andrew Strauss for his first-innings hundred there, and framed pictures of Matt Prior and Graham Onions shaking hands with the Queen.

Dotted around was the detritus of a sportsman's life: the good-luck messages, spare tickets, sunglasses, sponsors' gear and messages written on walls designed to inspire. A quote from Thomas Jefferson was on one wall: 'Nothing on earth can stop the man with the right mental attitude from reaching his goal; nothing on earth can help the man with the wrong mental attitude.' T.E. Lawrence was on another: 'All men dream but not equally. Those who dream by night in the dusty recesses of their minds wake in the day to find that it was vanity; but the dreamers of the day are dangerous men for they may act their dream with eyes open and make it possible.' England dared to dream and they were dangerous.

In the back room, where Andy Flower and his staff plotted and planned, and no doubt retired occasionally to bite nails to the quick, the noticeboard had a list of controllables and non-controllables. Can control: desire, respect, passion, commitment, patience, discipline, consistency, focus, preparation and trust. Can't control: weather, pitch, umpires, nets, schedule and, last of all, the Ashes.

In a way it was true that neither side was good enough to control the Ashes or their destiny. Neither team was quite good enough to get into a winning position and hold steady. Small things mattered – Monty Panesar's batting at Cardiff, the toss and the pitch at The Oval, the run outs measured in nanometres – almost more than anything else. Andrew Strauss had it right at the presentation ceremony when he said that when England were bad they were very bad and when they were good they were just about good enough. It was a long slog and a close run thing.

Historians may look back in time at the 2009 Ashes and puzzle over its outcome. After all, Australia scored eight hundreds to England's two and dominated the list of leading wicket-takers. By many statistical indicators, they, not England, should have won. But, in a way, such an illogical result was an entirely good thing for cricket, because the game had begun to be dominated by the statisticians to an unhealthy extent, so that players and spectators alike had become sucked into their importance, every irrelevant landmark applauded and recognised to the detriment of the bigger picture.

What matters more than bald numbers are the big moments and the match-winning performances and, on that measure, England had Australia's number. The five-for count was four to two in England's favour. At Lord's, England produced two match-winning performances, Andrew Strauss's first innings hundred and then Andrew Flintoff's astonishing spell on the final morning. At The Oval, Stuart Broad accepted Flintoff's mantle, with a match-winning spell on the second afternoon. Two bowl-ing spells from an ageing and a young all-rounder either side of the Thames made all the difference, along with Australia's fragility in the first innings: three times they suffered collapses, in the first innings at Lord's, Edgbaston and The Oval, and they were costly.

Statistics have long been aimed at Andrew Flintoff, an arrow I fired myself in a column before The Oval Test match. Whereas I make no apology for denying Flintoff greatness, there is no doubt that he has been a remarkable cricketer for England and his place in English cricketing history was assured by events at The Oval. What a delicious way to go out, and as he spoke at the end of the match it was a mature-sounding Flintoff who reflected on the great fortune of having enjoyed two Ashes-winning moments, moments shared with some special friends. Because of its place as the deciding venue of the summer, The Oval has given us many memorable exits over the years and the warmth with which Flintoff was sent on his way was as heartfelt as any send-off from the old ground.

Flintoff was the focus of the summer, but he was not the man of the summer. That accolade belonged to the captain, Andrew Strauss, who was immense throughout. Strauss is an impressive individual full stop: not many people would have been able to juggle the demands of captaining England in the Ashes, being father to a growing family, moving house, running a benefit and having a book ghosted. The job has got easier over the years as the ECB have offered more support, but this was still an impressive piece of compartmentalisation.

Strauss's strengths were as a leader not necessarily as a strate-gist. He is essentially a cautious captain, prone to thinking primarily about saving runs not taking wickets and about getting into a position from which defeat is impossible before thinking of victory. Those quibbles aside, it is clear that he is enormously respected by his team, as a leader, player and human being – even if they think him a trifle posh. His greatest attribute was his calmness, his ability not to get sidetracked by every crisis that came his way. His was a reassuring presence – at the top of the order and at the head of the unit.

The association he developed with Andy Flower was critical. The Flower–Strauss arrangement stands now with the Duncan Fletcher–Michael Vaughan alliance that was at the heart of the 2005 triumph. And since both Strauss and Flower are decent, grounded, modest men, it is unlikely they will let the 2009 vintage get carried away with victory as the 2005 side did.

As if relinquishing the Ashes were not enough, Australia suddenly found themselves demoted to fourth in the world in the ICC world rankings. It seemed a cruel thing but, in truth, it was merited. Try as hard as Ponting might, and boy did he try hard throughout the series to convince us otherwise, this was a moderate Australian team. Strauss had it right at Edgbaston, and it reflected England's confidence that he was prepared to say it straight out, that the Australian team lacked a certain 'aura'.

To those of us who had followed Australia since the beginning of the tour, Strauss was merely stating the obvious. Their players looked and sounded incredibly nervous in interview. It was hard to count the number of occasions a player had been asked for and the request was turned down because of the need to protect them. It was hard to think that Australian players of previous generations would have needed protecting or have been told what to say.

On the field, there were holes in their strategy everywhere. Once Phillip Hughes had been exposed, they had to do with a makeshift opening pair, Shane Watson looking no more like a permanent solution at the top of the order than Hughes. Mike Hussey's performance, despite his last-gasp century at The Oval, continued to plummet. Australia's attack was humdrum, Ben Hilfenhaus the best but hardly a leader of the attack in the Australian tradition. Mitchell Johnson disappointed. Nathan Hauritz surprised, but that Australia's selectors felt little enough faith to select him at The Oval spoke volumes.

At the end, it felt as if Australia was reacting in a very English way, turning in on itself after an Ashes defeat. Is Ponting the right man for the job? Who was responsible for the selections at The Oval? The media reaction had a touch of viciousness about it. Australians will have to get used to the notion that the period of dominance, of greatness, has gone. Which is not to say that they will not continue to be competitive.

Ponting, though, in this observer's estimation, had been harshly dealt with throughout the summer. He had become the pantomime villain for the crowd as they cheered every mis-field, every dismissal, every blow and booed every time he walked out to bat. But he had led his team well and spoken honestly and straightforwardly throughout. He deserved better.

The Ashes had, once again, helped to prove that Test cricket was alive and well and that, at least in England, the appetite for properly competitive five-day cricket was huge. The World Twenty20 was a distant memory. If there wasn't this time the astonishing sight of thousands being turned away at Old Trafford as four years previously, then there was no doubt that a 2009 ticket was a prized possession; a Wonka-like golden ticket. The matches were played to sell-outs, tickets bought, sold, bartered for and touted.

Giant screens played around the country, 7000 watching the denouement on one in Regent's Park. Commentators found new outlets for their enthusiasms, David 'Bumble' Lloyd's twitter site became a cult hit. The usual mixture of fly-by-night cricket celebrities and those with the game running through their blood found their way into the grounds. But with English grounds holding relatively small capacities and ticket prices hardly cheap, many 'ordinary' cricket supporters found themselves priced out of the contest.

If the 2009 series did not quite live up to 2005 then it was because the quality of the cricket was not as good. There were fewer great players on show, fewer great individual performances. The victories for both teams were on a massive scale, unlike four years before, only Cardiff providing a nail-biting finale. Nevertheless, the 2009 gave us much to be thankful for. Principally, it had drama: the last stand at Cardiff, the injuries to Kevin Pietersen and Andrew Flintoff, Flintoff's last hurrah at Lord's and the hoo-ha over his non-selection at Headingley, Langer's dossier, which ultimately was thrown right back in Australia's face, and the 'doctored' pitch at The Oval. Arise groundsman Bill Gordon, Lord of Lambeth!

The final image from the middle was that of Graeme Swann, wheeling away from his team-mates, once Mike Hussey's final inside edge had ended up in the hands of Alastair Cook at short-leg to confirm the destiny of the Ashes. He wheeled away and slid down on both knees, fists clenched, a look of ecstasy on his face. Had he known a happier moment?

In that moment I was reminded of something that the American scientist and sometime baseball writer, Stephen Jay Gould, wrote of a humdrum baseball player called 'Dusty' Rhodes who tasted a rare moment of greatness. 'We treasure the greats,' wrote Gould, 'but we hold special affection for the journeyman fortunate enough to taste greatness in an indelible moment of legitimate glory. We love Di Maggio because he was a paragon. We love Dusty Rhodes because he was a man like us. And his few days of majesty nurture a special hope that no ordinary person can deny. Any of us might get one chance for an act of transcendence – an opportunity to bake the greatest cake ever, to offer just the right support or advice, even save a life. And when that opportunity comes we do not want to succeed because we bought the lucky ticket in a lottery. Whatever the humdrum quality of our daily life, we yearn to know that, at some crucial moment, our special skills may render our presence exactly right and specially suited for that task required. Dusty Rhodes stands a symbol of that hope, that ever-present possibility.'

Swann is not exactly a journeymen, but nor is he a superstar of the game. Twenty-two days of cricket in 2009 asked questions of him that no other cricket, save another Ashes series, will ask of him again. The off-spinner from Nottinghamshire was not found wanting and nor, we hope when the time comes, will we.

The 2009 Ashes Statistical Record

1st Test, Sophia Gardens, Cardiff, on 8, 9, 10, 11, 12 July 2009
England 435 (K.P.Pietersen 69, P.D.Collingwood 64, M.J.Prior 56) and 252 for 9 (P.D.Collingwood 74)
Australia 674 for 6 dec (R.T.Ponting 150, M.J.North 125*, S.M.Katich 122, B.J.Haddin 121, M.J.Clarke 83)
Result: **Match Drawn**.

2nd Test, Lord's, London, on 16, 17, 18, 19, 20 July 2009
England 425 (A.J.Strauss 161, A.N.Cook 95) and 311 for 6 dec (M.J.Prior 61, P.D.Collingwood 54)
Australia 215 (M.E.K.Hussey 51) and 406 (M.J.Clarke 136, B.J.Haddin 80, M.G.Johnson 63, A.Flintoff 5 for 92)
Result: **England** won by 115 runs.

3rd Test, Edgbaston, Birmingham, on 30, 31 July, 1 (no play), 2, 3 August 2009
Australia 263 (S.R.Watson 62, J.M.Anderson 5 for 80) and 375 for 5 (M.J.Clarke 103*, M.J.North 96, M.E.K.Hussey 64, S.R.Watson 53)

England 376 (A.Flintoff 74, A.J.Strauss 69, S.C.J.Broad 55, I.R.Bell 53)
Result: **Match Drawn**.

4th Test, Headingley, Leeds, on 7, 8, 9 August 2009
England 102 (P.M.Siddle 5 for 21) and 263 (G.P.Swann 62, S.C.J.Broad 61, M.G.Johnson 5 for 69)
Australia 445 (M.J.North 110, M.J.Clarke 93, R.T.Ponting 78, S.R.Watson 51, S.C.J.Broad 6 for 91)
Result: **Australia** won by an innings and 80 runs.

5th Test, The Oval, London, on 20, 21, 22, 23 August 2009
England 332 (I.R.Bell 72, A.R.Strauss 55) and 373 for 9 dec (I.J.L.Trott 119, A.J.Strauss 75, G.P.Swann 63)
Australia 160 (S.M.Katich 50, S.C.J.Broad 5 for 37) and 348 (M.E.K.Hussey 121, R.T.Ponting 66)
Result: **England** won by 197 runs.

Series result: England won the series 2-1.
Men of the Series: M.J.Clarke (Australia) and A.J.Strauss (England).

SERIES AVERAGES

England – Batting and Fielding

Player	M	I	NO	HS	Runs	Ave	50	100	Ct/St
I.J.L.Trott	1	2	–	119	160	80.00	–	1	1
A.J.Strauss	5	9	–	161	474	52.67	3	1	4
K.P.Pietersen	2	4	–	69	153	38.25	1	–	1
G.P.Swann	5	8	1	63	249	35.57	2	–	1
A.Flintoff	4	7	1	74	200	33.33	1	–	1
M.J.Prior	5	9	1	61	261	32.62	2	–	11 /1
S.J.Harmison	2	3	2	19*	31	31.00	–	–	–
S.C.J.Broad	5	9	1	61	234	29.25	2	–	1
I.R.Bell	3	5	–	72	140	28.00	2	–	1
P.D.Collingwood	5	9	–	74	250	27.77	3	–	4
A.N.Cook	5	9	–	95	222	24.67	1	–	7
J.M.Anderson	5	8	2	29	99	16.50	–	–	2
R.S.Bopara	4	7	–	35	105	15.00	–	–	3
M.S.Panesar	1	2	1	7*	11	11.00	–	–	–
G.Onions	3	4	2	17*	19	9.50	–	–	–

England – Bowling

Player	Overs	Mdns	Runs	Wkts	Best	Ave	5wI	10wM
S.C.J.Broad	154.1	25	544	18	6-91	30.22	2	–
G.Onions	77.4	11	303	10	4-58	30.30	–	–
S.J.Harmison	43.0	10	167	5	3-54	33.40	–	–
G.P.Swann	170.2	30	567	14	4-38	40.50	–	–
J.M.Anderson	158.0	38	542	12	5-80	45.17	1	–
A.Flintoff	128.5	18	417	8	5-92	52.12	1	–

Also bowled: R.S.Bopara 8.2-1-44-0; P.D.Collingwood 18-1-76-1; M.S.Panesar 35-4-115-1.

Australia – Batting and Fielding

Player	M	I	NO	HS	Runs	Ave	50	100	Ct/St
M.J.Clarke	5	8	1	136	448	64.00	2	2	8
M.J.North	5	8	1	125*	367	52.42	1	2	3
R.T.Ponting	5	8	–	150	385	48.12	2	1	11
S.R.Watson	3	5	–	62	240	48.00	3	–	2
B.J.Haddin	4	6	–	121	278	46.33	1	1	15
S.M.Katich	5	8	–	122	341	42.62	1	1	6
M.E.K.Hussey	5	8	–	121	276	34.50	2	1	6
N.M.Hauritz	3	3	1	24	45	22.50	–	–	–
G.A.Manou	1	2	1	13*	21	21.00	–	–	3
B.W.Hilfenhaus	5	6	4	20	40	20.00	–	–	–
P.J.Hughes	2	3	–	36	57	19.00	–	–	1
P.M.Siddle	5	6	1	35	91	18.20	–	–	3
M.G.Johnson	5	6	–	63	105	17.50	1	–	–
S.R.Clark	2	3	–	32	38	12.67	–	–	–

Australia – Bowling

Player	Overs	Mdns	Runs	Wkts	Best	Ave	5wI	10wM
B.W.Hilfenhaus	180.5	40	604	22	4-60	27.45	–	–
P.M.Siddle	161.4	24	616	20	5-21	30.80	1	–
N.M.Hauritz	103.2	17	321	10	3-63	32.10	–	–
M.G.Johnson	162.1	15	651	20	5-69	32.55	1	–
S.R.Clark	47.0	12	176	4	4-131	44.00	–	–
M.J.North	67.3	13	204	4	4-98	51.00	–	–

Also bowled: M.J.Clarke 19-1-75-1; S.M.Katich 10-2-27-0; S.R.Watson 8-0-49-0.

BATTING RECORDS

Leading Run Scorers (300 runs or more)

Total	Player	Team	Average
474	A.J.Strauss	England	52.67
448	M.J.Clarke	Australia	64.00
385	R.T.Ponting	Australia	48.12
367	M.J.North	Australia	52.42
341	S.M.Katich	Australia	42.62

Hundreds

Score	Player	Team	Venue
161	A.J.Strauss	England	Lord's
150	R.T.Ponting	Australia	Cardiff
136	M.J.Clarke	Australia	Lord's
125*	M.J.North	Australia	Cardiff
122	S.M.Katich	Australia	Cardiff
121	B.J.Haddin	Australia	Cardiff
121	M.E.K.Hussey	Australia	The Oval
119	I.J.L.Trott	England	The Oval
110	M.J.North	Australia	Leeds
103*	M.J.Clarke	Australia	Birmingham

Highest Run Rate (over 66 runs per 100 balls, 50 runs scored)

Rate	Player	Team	Runs
83.27	G.P.Swann	England	249
81.81	M.J.Prior	England	261
72.72	A.Flintoff	England	200
72.67	S.C.J.Broad	England	234
69.50	B.J.Haddin	Australia	278
66.26	R.T.Ponting	Australia	385

Most Runs in Boundaries (170 or more)

Runs	Player	Team	Total	%age
260	A.J.Strauss	England	474	54.85
222	M.J.Clarke	Australia	448	49.55
204	R.T.Ponting	Australia	385	52.99
190	M.J.North	Australia	367	51.77
176	S.M.Katich	Australia	341	51.61

Partnerships

Hundred Partnerships (fig. denotes wicket)

239	2nd	S.M.Katich/R.T.Ponting	Australia	Cardiff
200	6th	M.J.North/B.J.Haddin	Australia	Cardiff
196	1st	A.J.Strauss/A.N.Cook	England	Lord's
185	5th	M.J.Clarke/M.J.North	Australia	Birmingham
185	6th	M.J.Clarke/B.J.Haddin	Australia	Lord's
152	5th	M.J.Clarke/M.J.North	Australia	Leeds
143	5th	M.J.Clarke/M.J.North	Australia	Cardiff
138	4th	K.P.Pietersen/P.D.Collingwood	England	Cardiff
127	3rd	R.T.Ponting/M.E.K.Hussey	Australia	The Oval
119	2nd	S.R.Watson/R.T.Ponting	Australia	Leeds
116	4th	A.J.Strauss/I.J.L.Trott	England	The Oval
108	8th	S.C.J.Broad/G.P.Swann	England	Leeds
102	2nd	A.J.Strauss/I.R.Bell	England	The Oval

Highest Partnership for Each Wicket

England

1st	196	A.J.Strauss/A.N.Cook	Lord's
2nd	102	A.J.Strauss/I.R.Bell	The Oval
3rd	81	A.J.Strauss/I.R.Bell	Birmingham
4th	138	K.P.Pietersen/P.D.Collingwood	Cardiff
5th	86	P.D.Collingwood/M.J.Prior	Lord's
6th	89	M.J.Prior/A.Flintoff	Birmingham
7th	52	A.Flintoff/S.C.J.Broad	Birmingham
8th	108	S.C.J.Broad/G.P.Swann	Leeds
9th	68	J.M.Anderson/G.P.Swann	Cardiff
10th	47	J.M.Anderson/G.Onions	Lord's

Australia

1st	86	S.R.Watson/S.M.Katich	The Oval
2nd	239	S.M.Katich/R.T.Ponting	Cardiff
3rd	127	R.T.Ponting/M.E.K.Hussey	The Oval
4th	42	M.E.K.Hussey/M.J.Clarke	Lord's
5th	185	M.J.Clarke/M.J.North	Birmingham
6th	200	M.J.North/B.J.Haddin	Cardiff
7th	70	M.J.North/M.G.Johnson	Leeds
8th	20	M.G.Johnson/P.M.Siddle	The Oval
9th	46	M.J.North/S.R.Clark	Leeds
10th	34	N.M.Hauritz/B.W.Hilfenhaus	Birmingham

BOWLING RECORDS

Leading Wicket Takers (12 or more)

Total	Player	Team	Average
22	B.W.Hilfenhaus	Australia	27.45
20	P.M.Siddle	Australia	30.80
20	M.G.Johnson	Australia	32.55
18	S.C.J.Broad	England	30.22
14	G.P.Swann	England	40.50
12	J.M.Anderson	England	45.17

Best Innings Analysis (5 wickets or more)

Figs	Player	Team	Venue
6-91	S.C.J.Broad	England	Leeds
5-21	P.M.Siddle	Australia	Leeds
5-37	S.C.J.Broad	England	The Oval
5-69	M.G.Johnson	Australia	Leeds
5-80	J.M.Anderson	England	Birmingham
5-92	A.Flintoff	England	Lord's

Best Match Analysis (8 wickets or more)

Figs	Player	Team	Venue
8-158	G.P.Swann	England	The Oval

Best Strike Rate (Max 60 balls per wicket, 10 wickets or more)

Rate	Player	Team	Wickets
46.6	G.Onions	England	10
48.5	P.M.Siddle	Australia	20
48.6	M.G.Johnson	Australia	20
49.3	B.W.Hilfenhaus	Australia	22
51.3	S.C.J.Broad	England	18

Most Economical Bowlers (100 overs or more)

Rate	Player	Team
3.10	N.M.Hauritz	Australia
3.23	A.Flintoff	England
3.32	G.P.Swann	England
3.34	B.W.Hilfenhaus	Australia
3.43	J.M.Anderson	England
3.52	S.C.J.Broad	England
3.81	P.M.Siddle	Australia
4.01	M.G.Johnson	Australia